About Careers Scotland

Careers Scotland offers a range of career planning and information services to enable people of all ages to maximise their career potential. As a national organisation, Careers Scotland has a clear and simple purpose – to help the people of Scotland secure the jobs of tomorrow.

Its aim is to make a difference by equipping people with the skills to make well-informed career decisions throughout their lives.

Careers Scotland operates centres throughout Scotland and can be contacted through the website www.careers-scotland.org.uk and on 0845 8 502 502.

It is part of Scottish Enterprise and Highlands and Islands Enterprise.

About Demos

Who we are

Demos is the think tank for everyday democracy. We believe everyone should be able to make personal choices in their daily lives that contribute to the common good. Our aim is to put this democratic idea into practice by working with organisations in ways that make them more effective and legitimate.

What we work on

We focus on six areas: public services; science and technology; cities and public space; people and communities; arts and culture; and global security.

Who we work with

Our partners include policy-makers, companies, public service providers and social entrepreneurs. Demos is not linked to any party but we work with politicians across political divides. Our international network – which extends across Eastern Europe, Scandinavia, Australia, Brazil, India and China – provides a global perspective and enables us to work across borders.

How we work

Demos knows the importance of learning from experience. We test and improve our ideas in practice by working with people who can make change happen. Our collaborative approach means that our partners share in the creation and ownership of new ideas.

What we offer

We analyse social and political change, which we connect to innovation and learning in organisations. We help our partners show thought leadership and respond to emerging policy challenges.

How we communicate

As an independent voice, we can create debates that lead to real change. We use the media, public events, workshops and publications to communicate our ideas. All our books can be downloaded free from the Demos website.

www.demos.co.uk

First published in 2006
© Demos
Some rights reserved – see copyright licence for details

ISBN 1 84180 161 5
Copy-edited by Julie Pickard, London
Typeset by utimestwo, Collingtree, Northants
Printed by Upstream, London

For further information and
subscription details please contact:

Demos
Magdalen House
136 Tooley Street
London SE1 2TU

telephone: 0845 458 5949
email: hello@demos.co.uk
web: www.demos.co.uk

Production Values

Futures for professionalism

Edited by
John Craig

DEMOS

DEM@S

Contents

Acknowledgements

First, I am extremely grateful to Careers Scotland for supporting this work. Thank you to Kate Hasson, Gordon MacDougall and the many members of staff at Careers Scotland who were so supportive throughout this process.

Thank you to all the contributors to this volume for their hard work. I have been surprised and delighted by your generosity and forbearance. In addition, those who attended our project seminar made an invaluable contribution and I am also grateful to the General Teaching Council for England for their contribution to our work in this area.

Thank you to the many other people who have contributed to this project, including Catherine Fieschi, Eddie Gibb, Sarah Gillinson, Sam Hinton-Smith, Julia Huber, Alyssa Joye, Anne Koch, Paul Miller, Duncan O'Leary, Simon Parker, Sophia Parker and Hannah Smith at Demos and Julie Pickard, our copy-editor. Thank you also to Paul Skidmore for wise counsel beyond the call of duty.

Finally, thanks most of all to Tom Bentley, for the usual editorial insight and for an incredible contribution to Demos.

John Craig
June 2006

Production values
Building shared autonomy

John Craig

The best solution is to do what the police say they need in order to protect the country from terrorism.

Tony Blair, 3 Nov 2005[1]

Public service reforms must be driven by the wishes of the users not the producers.

Tony Blair, 29 Nov 2005[2]

Professionals have never been more important nor under more pressure. Professionals 'profess' – promise – to deliver work of high standards and their promises keep us healthy and safe every day. But the promise of professionalism is struggling for credibility. As an institution, it faces a problem of legitimacy affecting not only doctors and lawyers but the success of governments and the freedom of their citizens. To solve this problem, we need to replace a schizophrenic view of professionals with a compelling account of their place in the public realm.

Professionalism is the form of work identity through which people win security and status in their work. At the same time, professionalism structures the exercise of power in everyday life. Professionalism sees parents leave their children with perfect strangers. We let professionals drug us. We give them licence to split up families and we send people to prison on their word. In the constitution of everyday life, therefore, distinctions between professionals and amateurs are more significant than those between executive and legislature or church and state.

In fact, we depend on professionalism more than ever. The professional mediation of competing demands increasingly trumps the political process. As fields from medicine to the arts become more specialised and separate, so politicians can seem to lack the deep knowledge and the legitimacy that judgement calls require. As a result, the burden of conflict resolution is shifting from political decisions to professional norms. Professionals play a greater role than ever in shaping our public realm and our daily lives.

More than the cleanliness of a hospital or the quality of resources in a school, it is the prompt, dependable work of professionals that is the key to our satisfaction with public services.[3] In the NHS, patients value the dignity and respect with which they are treated more than cleanliness, privacy or even the control of pain.[4] As a result, developing a compelling account of professionalism is crucially important both to government popularity and to the legitimacy of public authority.

Today, there is a danger that professionalism might become a victim of its own success, by outgrowing its own legitimacy. It is increasingly difficult for it to satisfy *either* individuals *or* society at large. In a society determined to make work pay, more individuals have strong career aspirations than ever before.[5] At the same time, as professionals grow in political significance, so there is greater scrutiny on their claims to status and expertise. Why are doctors able to deny people the right to die? What gives judges the right to interpret human rights? While professionalism has become *the* form of public mediation, the tensions this creates mean its own legitimacy is under threat.

The biggest barrier to renewing this professional legitimacy is the schizophrenia with which it is viewed. As professionals, people want autonomy and status but as consumers they expect slavish public servants, available 24/7. Equally, government is undecided whether to satisfy citizens as consumers or to work with them to *co-produce* services such as health and education. It is caught, as analysis of government rhetoric shows, between presenting them as saints or sinners – neutral experts or producer interests.

New professional legitimacy and culture will not be generated by setting professionals free to do as they please or by enslaving them to government targets and consumer demand. It cannot be designed into services by government blueprint. The 'choice agenda' does not create the kinds of high-quality, challenging conversations from which new shared protocols can emerge. The modest form of empowerment that choice represents continues to tie both citizens and professionals too closely to the script.[6]

New rationales for professional action will grow from practical collaboration between professionals and members of the public themselves. Today, this collaboration is all but absent from collective decision-making and it is time for government to match the rhetoric of partnership with concrete policy action. By giving professionals and citizens shared interests in working together to set local priorities, build shared optimism or tackle system failures, government can renew its agenda for public service reform from where it matters most, the everyday encounters between professionals and those they serve. It is this that can open up the black box of professional work and deliberation. In the process, it can achieve three vital political objectives: rebuilding government's relationship with the professions, tackling questions of work–life balance and investing in the legitimacy of public authority.

Understanding the professionals' game

The first task is to clarify our Janus-like approach to professionals. Today, government is torn between presenting professionals as neutral experts or producer interests. However, neither the selfless nor the selfish portraits of professionals can provide credible clues about how to respond to them in practice.

We should understand professionals not as saints or sinners but as they understand themselves – through their professions. Professional identity is constructed socially, through interactions with policy-makers, the public and other staff. It is through this professional identity – the shared habits and ideals of doctors, lawyers and teachers – and the interactions that build them that we should understand professionals.

Prevailing policy fails to do this because it conceptualises professionalism as an asset to be sold. We should instead understand professionalism like we do a sport or game – as something that possesses those who play it. In cricket, for example, players anticipate the ball and move towards it not because they decide to but simply because that is the game. Similarly, as staff develop 'a feel for the game', so their professionalism structures what counts as important and significant[7] – it becomes an end in itself.[8]

As an example, consider what the metaphor of a game suggests about attitudes to change. Imagine suggesting to a group of cricketers that one might play instead with a tennis ball.[9] They would surely balk at the idea, but not by arguing from first principles. 'It's just not cricket,' they would say. Similarly, communicating the idea that a profession might be *improved* is a slow and difficult process.

Equally, while government has long placed its faith in 'pressure and support' and 'earned autonomy', too often this comes across to professionals like trying to bribe a sportsman to throw a match. Organisations need to be able to address staff in the language of their own profession and to provide justifications that they will understand and value.[10] Engaging in terms of professionals' 'best interests' is no substitute for engaging with their profession – policy can nevertheless sound like 'an offer they can't refuse'.

Employers of all kinds need to adapt to a world in which the challenge is not to build professional loyalty but to live with its excess. Today, professionals are more absorbed in the game of their work than ever before. Most importantly, as we shall see, they need to shape opportunities for professionals to derive satisfaction and validation by working with the citizens they serve. This is the way to foster a sense of professional security that can survive and flourish in times of change.

Meeting public challenges

Alongside a new understanding of professionals, government needs a clear picture of the demands the public are making of professionalism. Where once professional authority seemed set in stone, today it has to be earned and this too must inform service design.

With the emergence of new technologies and the decline of deference, people have become more questioning of professionals than ever before. As individuals, we are more likely to check out the advice of a doctor online. As a society, we are more likely to share our intelligence about professional practice with both communities of interest and the national media.

This is happening for a range of reasons. First, consumer experiences in the private sector teach them to expect to access services when, how and where they choose. The imperative of personalisation – organising services around those they serve – increasingly impinges on all professionals. They must respond to clients well used to the idea that nothing is too much trouble. Second, as new divisions of labour continue to accompany economic growth, a growing proportion of work is paid work. As a result, some clients are becoming more passive recipients of the services they receive. Last, the internet revolution has begun to reverse the information asymmetries that used to be an inevitable feature of the relationship between professionals and clients. Alongside pressure from individual professionals, therefore, professionalism is under heavy pressure from society at large.

Helping professionals and citizens to work better together

The crucial mistake of government policy is to seek to meet the demands of professionals or of the public in isolation. Policy-makers have a sense that they must either cast their lot in with professionals or in with the public, so that they oscillate between the mantras of 'trust people' and 'trust the professionals'. However, the real challenge is to find design principles for services that bring professionals and citizens together to resolve the tensions between them. New visions of professionalism will emerge not from legislation alone but from real work between professionals and those they serve. While every politician fears being a 'statist' or a 'producerist', we nevertheless need policies that address the needs of professionals *as well as* consumers.

Public services need to give professionals and clients a common interest in working together. Too often, we conceptualise public services as a boxing ring, and seek to support people by putting 'choice advisers' in their corner, before sending them into battle with professionals.[11] It is hardly surprising that this does not generate new terms on which their relationship can flourish. The location of public encounters with professionals should feel less like being in a boxing ring and more like getting stuck in a lift – where each side has to work to question their assumptions and make conversation.

Examples of these locations serve not as a blueprint for a new professionalism but as snapshots of the kinds of places from which it might emerge. In schooling, participatory budgeting gives teachers and parents greater freedom to pursue their aims, but only if they work together to agree priorities.[12] In the NHS, where investments can be made in sources of good health – from community gyms to walking clubs – doctors and patients can work together to improve health. In local authorities, where commissioning strategies can switch resources into prevention, all kinds of professionals and publics can unlock shared interests in self-help. Lastly, across the public realm, if we could assess the levels of hope and collective efficacy on a given issue, professionals could focus on public relationships as themselves vital resources in getting the job done.[13]

In other words, designing for a new professionalism would focus attention on a clear set of questions. How can social enterprises provide blank sheets of paper on which professionals and publics might re-cast their relationships to common benefit? How can new forms of local democracy compel professionals and communities to work better together? Lastly, how can a focus on prevention and self-help enable the autonomy of professionals and of those they serve to grow together?

As we at Demos look to find answers to these questions and to assemble this set of design principles, the essays in this collection provide an invaluable set of starting points. In particular, they show that the everyday encounters between professionals and citizens must help them to build relationships capable of responding to four challenges:

○ the information revolution
○ new personal demands
○ the dilemma of corporate professionalism
○ demands for cross-functionality.

The information revolution

The information revolution is changing the terms of relationships between professionals and their clients.[14] As new opportunities allow people to become their own journalists, physicians and travel agents, so their attitudes to professionals are changing.

The paradigmatic example of this cultural motif seems to be the television programme *Faking It*, in which in three weeks a seamstress learns to pass herself off as a video director, a classical cellist as a DJ. Today, all kinds of professional authority are up for grabs. In medicine, for example, the tyranny of Google ranking means that official NHS advice must vie with that of Pampers and Mothercare for the attention of parents.

Professionals are responding to this trend in two key ways. First, they are opening up access to their ranks. For example, Teach First works as a kind of *Faking It* for education, with able graduates given ten weeks to learn the ropes before being placed in some of the most challenging classrooms in London. Equally, as our work with Careers Scotland shows, organisations are increasingly determined to grow leaders from within their own ranks. In the words of one proud Careers Scotland employee: 'In terms of a professional, you tend to think of someone with a university degree, but I feel like I am a professional too. I've become a professional.' Across our public services, people who used to be known as para-professionals – from community safety officers to nurses to classroom assistants – are relishing new opportunities to join the professional ranks. How professions and professional associations respond to this new diversity is a key question for the future.

Second, a focus on enabling self-help is beginning to supersede the idea that professionals have all the answers. This is a point that Richard Reeves and John Knell and Charles Leadbeater make very powerfully in their essays. As Leadbeater argues: 'Motivation is the new medicine.' Enabling self-help implies not simply a shift in priorities but the development of a new professional vocabulary and skill set. Professionals have to be able to explain issues to their clients in terms that they understand and which invite questions and participation. They have also to learn to inspire clients to help themselves.

In his essay, Jay Rosen shows that journalism is firmly ahead of this curve as a crisis in journalism shifts journalists' perceptions of their role. Where once journalists themselves were defenders of the public interest, today journalists increasingly seek to help the public to defend itself. As other essays in this collection show, where journalism is leading, many other professions are following. From career planning to the arts, a more equal relationship with the public is increasingly both a fact of life and a defining professional value.

New personal demands

Zygmunt Bauman argued that 'modern organisation is a contraption designed to make human actions immune from what the actors believe and feel privately'.[15] However, today our experiences of work have come full circle, with professional and personal values more closely connected than ever before. While for some this is a source of satisfaction, for others it can create stress and exhaustion. In order to support professional work, we need to help people to build new relationships between their personal and professional lives.

The fusion of personal and professional roles has been driven by demands from both employers and professionals. As systems of services have grown in complexity in recent years, employers have sought to shift from mixes of rules-based and professional regulation to looser, values-led coordination. Today, fewer professionals have formal autonomy and few have been able to reserve the exclusive right of self-regulation. However, as Laura Empson points out in her essay, organisations have nevertheless sought to sustain a professional culture, focusing on informal professional ethics and norms.

At the same time, professionals themselves also seem to have worked with the grain of this shift. As work becomes more central to our ambitions, people are identifying increasingly closely with their professional roles. Equally, in the absence of formal control, a focus on informal values helps professionals to retain influence over how work is done, if not over what is done. In recent years, therefore, the idea that the personal is professional has been pushed by both staff and employers.

However, the result is that professional work involves more emotional labour than ever before – organisational coordination depends on winning hearts as well as minds. For example, as our research on teaching describes,[16] over any two-year period, 40 per cent of teachers will experience 'major stress'[17] and in any given year 40 per cent of headteachers visit their doctor as a result of stress.[18] When professionals identify so intimately with their work, it can be almost impossible 'switch off' when it is time to go home. Work-related stress is growing across many professions and while we may work fewer hours, this does not mean that we are less exhausted.[19] From the former leader of a teachers' union who recently broke down in tears on stage[20] to the teacher who remortgaged her house to keep open a unit at her school,[21] professional work tugs at the heart strings more than ever. As professionals begin to develop responses, they are shaping new opportunities for reflection and new rituals through which to share their emotional burden. However, as changing demographics begin to make recruitment and retention a key professional problem, policy-makers and employers will have to face this challenge too. Professionalism must satisfy consumer demand but we also need a sustainable professionalism, and the search for it is beginning to intensify.

The dilemma of corporate professionalism

The rise of the knowledge economy is creating new common interests for professional staff and their employers. However, as these organisations encroach on territory from which they were once excluded they are generating both optimism and anxiety. In response, employers, professionals and citizens will have to re-cast their relationships.

In his essay, Tom Wilson describes the way in which small, professional unions are managing to buck the prevailing trend and secure rapid growth. As professional development becomes the key to the fortunes of both individual staff and to whole companies, he argues that unions may be finding a new purpose. Far from being a check on growth in the short term, unions may be instrumental in enabling long-term investment. Unions may become valuable to their members not for the rewards they secure today but for the opportunities they create for tomorrow. This suggests that trade unions and professional associations may find new ways to connect their members' interests with the public interest.

However, for Kipping, Kirkpatrick and Muzio, the idea that professionals might work in partnership with their employers forgets the huge power of multinational corporations. They argue that in the knowledge economy some firms increasingly win staff loyalty and commitment by 'mimicking' professional structures and practices. For them, while such partnerships create the experience of professionalism, they rob staff of any real power.

This dilemma of corporate professionalism is an extremely important one. For example, it is picked up in detail in our work on the futures of the career planning profession. As Careers Scotland looks to make the most of professional self-regulation in driving up the standards of its service, it is playing more of an active professional role. For its staff, the organisation is increasingly the site of professional dialogue. However, to legitimate this shift, it is also seeking to give professionals greater control of the development of best practice and organisational policy. This kind of negotiation between professions and organisations will be of vital importance across many sectors in coming years. How far can trade unions and employers become sites of professional dialogue? And just when do staff feel that they have become professionals only in name?

Demands for cross-functionality

Lastly, a whole range of professions are experiencing fundamental shifts in their centres of gravity. Numerous professions are increasingly defined as much by their locality and their client groups as by their expertise. While this is challenging terrain for professionals, it is opening up vital dialogue with those they serve.

As Estelle Morris and Keith Brumfitt make clear in their essay, the personalisation agenda depends on professional reform. Equally, across children's services, local responsibilities for workforce strategy and approaches to collaboration are enabling considerable national variation. As this grows the need for deep local reflection about what it means to be a teacher or social worker *in* Birmingham or *in* Knowsley, so we may be witnessing the birth of local professionalism. Just as professional dialogue is spreading into organisations, so it is advancing into local politics and policy-making. Michael Bichard addresses this directly in his essay, contrasting the way professionals approach this dialogue in local and national government. How far can professions bear local diversity? What new approaches to organisation might this diversity generate?

Growing professional autonomy

As these challenges show, professionalism must contend with new sources of equality, personal stress, dilemmas of corporatism and pressures for diversity. However, professionals have long shown their ability to adapt, most often to avoid changes enforced from beyond their ranks. The challenge now is to unlock that adaptive capacity for the common good and we can do this by changing the circumstances under which they encounter the public.

For too long, government has felt that in seeking to deliver on its own promises, it must choose between casting its lot in with professionals *or* citizens. This is a mistake that frustrates government's own ambitions and which systematically shuts down opportunities to re-cast professional relationships. These essays show the potential of finding ways to encourage people to work together to help professional and citizen autonomy to grow together. They suggest that a new professionalism will emerge not from the words of policy-makers or researchers, but from collaborative work between professionals and those they serve.

While finding a consistent and compelling account of the role of professionals is increasingly vital to public service reform, it may also be rising up the party political agenda. Recent reports have suggested a Conservative opposition looking to 'woo public sector professionals'.[22] Public sector professionals are no more loyal to the Labour Party than the population as a whole[23] and are also an important source of electoral credibility and governmental success. The race to establish a compelling political narrative about professionals may be beginning in earnest.

To win that race, policy-makers need to shape everyday encounters between professionals and citizens that enable them to grow their autonomy together. In the process, they can help people to develop new relationships with work, new approaches to the exercise of authority in everyday life and new energy in reforming public services. They must engage in a 'double devolution' that empowers citizens *and* professionals.[24]

Notes

1   T Blair, speaking in the House of Commons, 3 Nov 2005.
2   T Blair, in a speech to the Confederation of British Industry, 29 Nov 2005.
3   MORI, *Public Service Reform: Measuring & understanding customer satisfaction* (London: MORI, 2002), see www.mori.com/publications/rd/opsr.pdf (accessed 25 May 2006).
4   MORI, *Frontiers of Performance in the NHS* (London: MORI, 2004), see www.mori.com/publications/bp/frontiers2.shtml (accessed 25 May 2006).
5   M Rose, 'Career outlook and reasons for having paid work, 1985–2001', 2003, see www.bath.ac.uk/~hssmjr/trajex/download/execrep.doc (accessed 25 May 2006).

6   C Leadbeater, *Personalisation through Participation: A new script for public services* (London: Demos, 2004).

7   P Bourdieu, *Practical Reason* (Palo Alto, CA: Stanford University Press, 1998).

8   In particular, professionalism is what Carse calls an 'infinite game', in which the point is not to win but to keep on playing. JP Carse, *Finite and Infinite Games: A vision of life as play and possibility* (New York: Ballatine Books, 1987).

9   This example is based on that of the 'fourth strike' in baseball, in S Cavell, *The Claim of Reason* (Oxford: Oxford University Press, 1999).

10 Thanks to Dr Alan Finlayson for help in clarifying this point.

11 Department for Education and Skills, *Higher Standards, Better Schools for All*, 2005, see www.dfes.gov.uk/publications/schoolswhitepaper/ (accessed 25 May 2006).

12 J Craig, *Schools Out: Can teachers, social workers and health staff learn to live together?* (London: The Hay Group, 2004).

13 P Skidmore and J Craig, *Start with People: How community organisations put citizens in the driving seat* (London: Demos, 2005).

14 C Leadbeater and P Miller, *The Pro-Am Revolution: How enthusiasts are changing our economy and society* (London: Demos, 2004).

15 Z Bauman, *Alone Again: Ethics after certainty* (London: Demos, 1994).

16 Based on research with the General Teaching Council of England.

17 Research by Teacherline, quoted in C Bunting, 'Stress on the emotional landscape', *Times Educational Supplement*, 10 Nov 2000, see www.tes.co.uk/section/story/?section=Archive&sub_section=Briefing&story_id =340592&Type=0 (accessed 22 May 2006).

18 Research by the National Association of Headteachers, quoted in M Jarvis, 'Teacher stress: a critical review of recent findings and suggestions for future research directions', *Stress News* 14, no 1 (Jan 2002).

19 M Bunting, *Willing Slaves: How the overwork culture is ruling our lives* (London: Harper Collins, 2004).

20 See http://news.bbc.co.uk/1/hi/education/4916004.stm (accessed 25 May 2006).

21 Thanks to Emma Westcott of the General Teaching Council for this example. See http://news.bbc.co.uk/1/hi/england/hampshire/4920430.stm (accessed 25 May 2006).

22 P Wintour, 'Tories plan to woo public sector professionals with more freedom', *Guardian*, 12 May 2006, see www.guardian.co.uk/guardianpolitics/story/0,,1773081,00.html (accessed 25 May 2006).

23 MORI, *Disaffected Labour* (London: MORI, 2005), see www.mori.com/publications/sa/disaffected-labour.shtml (accessed 25 May 2006).

24 Speech by D Miliband to the National Council of Voluntary Organisations, 21 Feb 2006, see www.odpm.gov.uk/index.asp?id=1163772 (accessed 25 May 2006).

Essay summaries

Learning from the professionals

The new cultural professionals
Sam Jones

The public is coming to play an ever-more important part in cultural policy and thinking. Where, in the past, cultural provision was based on cultural professionals' own expertise, a new role for cultural professionals is emerging. Using their expertise to enable and explain, rather than deliver, cultural professionals help us to navigate and engage with the world around us in new ways.

Culture grows from the complex interactions between artists and audiences. Today, audiences are more proactive than ever before and expect to be able to express their own creativity. In this context, new cultural professionals are emerging who specialise in enabling artistic dialogue. In the process, these professionals are becoming 'explorers in the public interest', using their own ingenuity to enable artists and audiences to grow together. They are building ambitious artistic partnerships that span the public realm and building on the democratic significance of culture. In response, cultural policy should acknowledge the breadth of cultural activities and engage with them on their own terms.

The activist police force
Charlie Edwards

The police are very far from being 'the last great unreformed public service'. From the introduction of community support officers to a new emphasis on community policing, police officers are seeking to become known local figures capable of reassuring and engaging with the public. This is a very significant shift.

Over the last two years, Demos has involved over 150 police officers in 'futures thinking' work looking at the changing nature of policing. The results suggest that, beyond the various operational changes, a deep cultural change is beginning to spread across the police force. Today, police officers are becoming more proactive – they are happier to work in partnership with other agencies and increasingly confident in using their own ingenuity for the public good.

Given the history of the police, this is a significant achievement in professional reform. Police officers have good reason to be suspicious of political interference and to be wary of 'mission creep'. However, as they grow into new roles, officers in the force are learning to combine their core duties with the need to work as 'activist professionals'.

The career planning professional
John Craig

The dramatic changes that have taken place at Careers Scotland in recent years show the power of allying organisational reform to professional dialogue. Careers Scotland is attempting to develop a new kind of relationship between professionals and their employer.

Career planning professionals have had to come to terms with the idea that public scrutiny and collective responsibility are now non-negotiable elements of their work. They are also learning to work in equal partnership with their clients and to organise their services around their needs. As part of the process, opportunities for sense-making professional conversations have been vitally important.

In return, Careers Scotland is creating new opportunities for all its staff to professionalise, driving up the standard of the services provided to the public. It is also opening up the development of policy and best practice to contributions from its staff. As Careers Scotland develops this new professional settlement, it is tackling the dilemma of corporate professionalism. To what extent can organisations become the site of professional dialogue? Careers Scotland is beginning to find out.

The lead professional in children's services
Estelle Morris and Keith Brumfitt

Children's services face an organisational challenge with a professional solution. 'Lead professionals' can help to integrate provision for our most vulnerable children and to provide a single point of contact for them and their parents. To do so, they must work across a range of services *and* have much more direct day-to-day contact with children. This is a demanding new professional role but one with huge potential to help to achieve deep cultural change.

Lead professionals will challenge professional tribalism and the authority of professional expertise. To do so effectively, they will have to model deep ethical commitment that can span professional loyalties and develop real diplomatic skill. Their task is to help orient organisations around the needs of each child and to build professional commitment to personalisation across children's services.

Lead professionals will take account of not only the views of professional colleagues but those of young people themselves. In the process, they will seek to model the new professional culture it is their task to help build.

The plan is dead; long live the planner
Peter Bradwell and Inderpaul Johar

The complexity of today's communities fundamentally challenges the planning profession. Where once planners could take individual responsibility for shaping local blueprints, today they face a range of new pressures. On the one hand, new national imperatives of environmental sustainability and housing stock growth encourage planners to take up command and control of the planning process.

On the other, demands for local democracy encourage planners to shape a much more open and participative planning process.

To resolve this tension, planning is urgently in need of professional reform. This process amounts to a choice among a range of possible scenarios for the future of planning. From the planner as judge, explicitly independent and free from scrutiny, to the planner as networker, seeking to connect and unite competing local interests, these scenarios raise deep questions about the planner's role. As Demos begins a research project in this area, we aim to explore and develop these scenarios and use them to build a consensus about planning in the years ahead.

Towards DIY professionalism: stress in the teaching profession
John Craig

For teachers, stress is an increasingly important issue, but for policy-makers stress can seem like a good thing – a sign of 'challenge' and 'stretch'. However, these two perspectives draw on very different notions of stress. In teaching, stress is increasingly about being stretched to breaking point, and its implications are becoming very serious for individual teachers and for the profession as a whole.

This rise in stress in teaching in the UK outstrips both other professions and other countries. Its causes can be traced back to particular features of our teaching profession. For teachers, their profession is becoming a DIY professionalism, which they themselves must define and build – they must work to justify their own status and authority every day.

For those teachers lacking great confidence or resilience, this creates professional stress in a range of ways. Teachers are experiencing growing emotional stress through intense relationships with work, growing intellectual stress through initiative overload and growing physical stress from a job that is more demanding than ever. As a result, finding sustainable forms of professionalism for teachers is a pressing priority.

Professional innovation

Journalism is itself a religion (and the faith is being tested)
Jay Rosen

Journalism is like a religion: it has a priesthood, an orthodoxy and a foundation myth. The myth that surrounds the Watergate scandal has become a blanket justification for the work of journalists, 'in the name of the public's right to know'. In a story that was once about politics, heroic journalists now take centre stage. However, while this myth continues to grow, its salience as a set of guiding principles for journalism is failing. For too long, the religion of the press has protected the profession from having to justify its work in the language of democratic politics.

Journalists have sought to combine innocence (we do just the facts journalism) and the power (we do make a difference journalism), but these two are increasingly incompatible. In a world where the public itself can produce media as well as consume it, both the neutrality and the influence of journalists are being called into question. In response, journalists are seeking to build a new professional code, whose new god is the public. While journalism may be in crisis, if journalists can find new ways to involve and empower 'the people formerly known as the audience', we may yet find ways for the freedoms of press and public to grow together.

Tomorrow's workers, yesterday's trades
Tom Wilson

Small professional unions are bucking the trend of membership decline and achieving rapid growth. In part, the growth of professional unions is inevitable as professional and managerial work grows as a fraction of the economy. However, in some cases unions that focus on professional issues are growing at the expense of others.

These professional unions seem to be thriving because they have found an interest that they, their members and employers all share: professional development. In the knowledge economy, company productivity and staff prospects alike depend on how much people learn through work and develop new skills. Professional unions are shaping a new role at the heart of this professional learning, and it is one their members increasingly appreciate.

This may prove a significant shift. From being seen as drivers of cost in the short term to firms and economies, this may help unions to win recognition of their role as drivers of investment for the long term. Equally, as individuals seek to cope with a rapidly changing economy and world of work, unions may come to be seen as helping people to achieve their ambitions tomorrow as much as they defend their professional status today.

Governance and the analytic institution
Helen Morgan

This essay discusses the profession of psychoanalysis and psycho-therapy. It uses a powerful metaphor to describe an ideal for the profession's organisation. For a baby, the capacity to be alone is a crucial part of its development. This happens through the infant being able to be alone in *the presence of* the mother. The baby is 'alone', but the mother is reliably present to protect and look after it.

In the same way, we can think of governance within the profession of psychoanalysis and psychotherapy as this 'other' in the presence of which professionals must be able to practise 'alone'. Given the intimacy and privacy on which their work depends, getting this balance right is vitally important. Professional governance, in other words, must enable without intruding.

However, this relationship can go wrong. The anxious mother can intrude on the play of her child, preventing him or her from learning. Equally, governance can become paranoid and intrusive. Morgan argues that it is for the senior members of the profession to engage proactively with government and seek to ensure that this paranoia is kept in check.

Promoting the global accountancy professional
Allan Blewitt

The Association of Chartered Certified Accountants (ACCA) is now represented in 170 countries and is seeking to become the leading professional association in the sector. In the process, it must help accountancy to recover from the scandals of Enron, WorldCom and Parmalat, which have all challenged its reputation.

To achieve this objective, ACCA has placed great emphasis on the idea that global professional responsibility goes far beyond financial probity. ACCA argues that accountants have a role in regulating global financial systems and in ensuring that they function in the public interest. It seeks to promote values of professionalism, diversity and democracy, functioning as a 'safety net for the public interest' across the world.

In the process, ACCA is seeking to make professionalism and professional values a key resource in helping accountants to resolve the ethical dilemmas they face every day. Alongside its regulatory role, ACCA is establishing a key developmental function, seeking to expand opportunities to join the global professional ranks.

Double devolution: how to put the amateurs in charge
Nick Aldridge and Astrid Kirchner

The 'double devolution' agenda will focus attention on third sector organisations as gatekeepers of community involvement. Under this spotlight, the professionalism of their staff will be crucially important.

However, professionalism has long been a guilty secret in the third sector, with organisations wary of bureaucracy and of diverting investment from the front line. The lack of investment in professional development has created a skills gap, to which business schools, training providers and acevo (Association of Chief Executives of Voluntary Organisations) are beginning to respond.

This response is crucially important. Third sector organisations need to learn to set high professional standards alongside their ability to involve volunteers. It is this pro-am culture, involving people pursuing amateur activities to professional standards, that helps third sector organisations to create both innovation and efficiency.

However, the balance this culture requires is a difficult one to strike. Risk aversion, bureaucratic funding processes and challenges to third sector legitimacy pressure organisations to professionalise at the expense of voluntary involvement. Third sector organisations will need determination to get this balance right and for their part government must enable them to do so.

Professionals in partnership
Laura Empson

As the governance of the legal profession shifts its legal form from a partnership model to a corporate model, it has sparked a keen debate about the significance of corporate professionalism. For example, commentators have suggested that the need to satisfy external shareholders will undermine lawyers' professional ethos.

However, professionalism is not simply being colonised by corporate interests. Partnership is most fundamentally a state of mind not a legal form and managers can do a great deal to ensure that it survives and thrives in a changing world. Where partnership does survive, the partnership ethos has the vital capacity to hold the worst excesses of corporatism in check.

Even as a firm dispenses with partnership as a form of governance, managers can sustain a partnership ethos. To do so, they must ensure that they socialise professionals in the right way, foster systems that reward ethical behaviour and build organisational structures that ensure decisions are consensual and taken in the long-term interests of the firm and the public.

Overly controlled or out of control? Management consultants and the new corporate professionalism
Matthias Kipping, Ian Kirkpatrick and Daniel Muzio

There is a suggestion that the shared interests of management consultants and their employers have made professionalisation unnecessary. In fact, management consultants have failed to professionalise because large firms in the sector have sought to resist and stifle the process.

Organisations like McKinsey have built a brand by mimicking the professional cultures of law firms while denying their staff equivalent autonomy. The result is that while the image of management consultancies is protected by their professional reputation, management consultants themselves work in an increasingly bureaucratic and tightly regulated environment.

This is part of a shift towards a *corporate professionalism* in which organisations themselves become the main locus of professional exercise, closure and regulation. This shift raises tough questions about individuals' experiences of consultancy and about the regulation of the sector. It remains to be seen how consultants' morale stands up to corporate professionalism and how effective this 'soft regulation' will be in ensuring that scandals such as Enron are avoided in the future.

Futures for professionalism

The profession of public service

Michael Bichard

In previous decades, local government was extremely suspicious of generalists and authorities were organised along tribal professional lines. In contrast, the civil service nationally has a history of tremendous faith in the capacity of the gifted amateur. However, despite this contrast in organisational approach, what they shared was a lack of collective responsibility.

Today, while the civil service is seeking to professionalise, local authorities are working to break down professional silos. And while in the past professional loyalty superseded all others, today this is also changing. More and more staff acknowledge a genuine sense of responsibility to the organisation and the public that they serve.

As this shift continues, the question is whether there is now a case for establishing a single public service profession in the UK. Such a move would surely encourage a free flow of people and ideas across sectors and across tiers of government. While many vested interests are ranged against this suggestion, we should aspire to public services that minimise the barriers to mobility and innovation. It is an idea whose time has come.

Production by the masses: professionals and postindustrial public services
Charles Leadbeater

Many professionals are demoralised and feel at odds with the systems within which they work. This is because they are trapped within semi-industrial service systems that seek to deliver ready-made solutions to passive customers. In response, we need an entirely new set of design principles to guide public service reform over the next two decades.

However, professional reform is a challenging endeavour. Professionals can quickly become defensive, lapsing into specialist language that seeks to preserve their monopolistic position. The danger of professionalism is that it can become an end in itself and that professionals can come to dominate how we understand social problems and how we seek to solve them.

Our aim should be to create postindustrial public services that are more collaborative, networked and distributed. Public institutions and professionals should educate us towards self-help and self-reliance. In health, motivation is the new medicine and in education we need to develop independent learners with a hunger for knowledge. As a result, professionals need to learn to act as persuaders, counsellors and campaigners, encouraging people to acquire the skills to look after themselves more effectively.

Gender and professionalism
Hilary De Lyon

While women now make up the majority of many professions, they continue to be seriously underrepresented in their upper echelons. This essay asks why achieving professional equality has proved so much more than a question of numbers and looks at what government, professional associations and professionals themselves can do to develop professional structures that are open and fair.

The most significant barriers to professional leadership for women are lack of flexible working, prejudice and professional cultures. As demographic change begins to make professional recruitment and retention a pressing public issue, pressure to remove these barriers is likely to grow. However, as the history of many professions shows, while social change may create opportunities, to exploit them requires dedication and persistence. As part of this process, both government legislation and pressure from professional associations have important roles to play. However, women themselves face a dilemma between succeeding in professions as they are and developing a new vision of professionalism as it could be.

Strengthening professionalism: ethical competence as a path towards the public good
Andy Friedman

In seeking to regulate professional services, governments face a choice between two solutions: market forces and professional ethics. The market forces solution focuses attention on removing monopolistic barriers to competition while the professional ethics solution focuses attention on education and training, professional associations and professionals themselves. The second solution has been all but completely neglected by the current government.

However, particular features of professional services make market forces an imperfect form of regulation. Information asymmetry between professionals and their clients means that consumer power is strictly limited. At the same time, because professional services are purchased infrequently, consumer preferences do not evolve over time in the way they do in other markets.

As a result, government should look again at professional ethics as a way to regulate professional services. It should encourage professional associations to do more to increase professional development and to ensure professional standards. For their part, professional associations must ensure that they review, develop and promote their ethical codes.

Good work and professional work

Richard Reeves and John Knell

Professional identity has been grounded in good qualifications and good collective organisation – in the future it will need to be based on 'good work'. In the past, professions defined themselves through their entry requirements and collective organisation. However, as this kind of exclusive professional status becomes harder to defend, professions will have to build on two other important features of their identity.

First, professional ethics have become more important than ever. It may profit the professional to prescribe a particular drug or to be economical with the truth and this remains a vital test of professional integrity.

Second, professionals must be judged in terms of the impact of their work. They should aspire to doing 'good work' – where excellence and ethics meet. Public interest, in other words, will increasingly become *the* test of professionalism. To respond to this shift, professionals need to re-connect with the deeper roots of their authority: why, how and to what end they work.

Learning from the
professionals

1. The new cultural professionals

Sam Jones

The public is coming to play an ever-more important part in cultural policy and thinking. Where, in the past, cultural provision has been based on cultural professionals' own expertise, a new role for the cultural professional is emerging. Using their expertise to enable and explain, rather than deliver, cultural professionals can help us navigate and engage with the world around us in ways that can re-invigorate our society.

Changing contexts

As other essays in this collection show, we – the public – are placing changing demands on the professionals whose services we use. We exercise greater individuality in what we choose to eat and wear; we demand more personalised services from our public organisations and institutions; and we are much readier to complain when we do not get the service we expect.

The same is true of our cultural choices. Our iPods are our personal orchestras, and at exhibitions we expect to be able to interact with displays and have the right to comment on them afterwards. After years of meeting economic targets and fulfilling social criteria – so-called instrumental demands – such developments seem to offer cultural professionals a new opportunity. Culture is, after all, something that is born of us and the way that we respond to each other – it is up to cultural professionals to draw that out.

Recent policy reflects this new, more creative role. The Minister for Culture, David Lammy, has spoken recently of a 'cultural democracy', defined by 'the quality of the relationship between cultural professionals and the public'.[1] John Holden's *Cultural Value and the Crisis of Legitimacy* presents the need for a new democratic mandate for culture, based on how people engage in our culture, and how cultural institutions work to encourage and build that engagement.[2] Cultural professionals, he argues, 'have a legitimate role in shaping public opinion and encouraging and validating public debate'.

However, there is a tension. As the public, our interest in investigating a particular aspect of culture is very much our own, but we also expect the professional to pique that interest. However, for the cultural professional this can easily feel like dumbing down, shifting their role from expert to entertainer. According to one commentator, museums, for example, are caught invidiously between two, hackneyed political stools of our day: 'on the one hand the market-driven utilitarianism of the right which has forced them to justify their existence in crude economic terms; on the other, the guilt-ridden orthodoxies of the cultural left'.[3]

Both the political demands for accessibility and the instrumental demands of politicians and funders frame the cultural professional's role as responsive rather than creative. Their expertise is put at the service of other agendas. This is missing a trick. As politicians champion community and the agendas of inclusion and cross-cultural awareness dominate current policy more generally, it is the cultural sector that can provide the answers. Far from responding to the agenda of others, cultural professionals are in a position to address some of the key issues society faces. However, for cultural professionals to take on this new role, they too must respond to the changes around them. Below, three examples show how the expertise of the cultural professional is the lifeblood of the 'cultural democracy' of which the Minister for Culture has spoken.

Redefining the cultural professional

While we have been downloading songs to our mobile phones and voting for which building should be saved by the BBC's *Restoration*, culture has emerged as a new medium of engagement. While only 61.3 per cent voted in the 2005 general election, 80 per cent of Britons engage in cultural activities annually. Very simply, the public value cultural engagement. However, if – as the Minister for Culture believes it should – cultural engagement is to be given *democratic* meaning, then cultural professionals in the public sector face new challenges. The challenge is to generate public value – to 'challenge the ends of politics, not just the means', and become 'explorers who are commissioned by society to . . . search for better ways of doing things'.[4] To do so, cultural professionals must:

O extend the ways in which they collaborate with and engage with their publics
O use their own creativity to work together to create cultural value
O create a more widespread and equal understanding of culture as something that is born of public engagement, rather than given or delivered.

In so doing, cultural professionals can build our capacity to enjoy cultural activity in more meaningful and expressive ways. At the same time, they can create a new role for themselves as facilitators of that enjoyment.

Emerging models of engagement

Current trends in society may have given cultural consumption renewed significance and cultural professionals are becoming increasingly skilled in building on this significance. Cultural consumption is becoming central to an increasingly 'play-centred' society:

> *[A] play culture regards the arts as creating the good player. It promotes the arts as a means of developing one's subjective agency, emotional literacy and aliveness to forms of expression.*

> *By producing or consuming culture, individuals face the*
> *information age with renewed vitality and imagination. For*
> *players, art is not a private pleasure, but an input into the daily*
> *practices of creative living: keeping organisations healthy,*
> *networks flexible, relationships vibrant and life-options*
> *multiplying.*[5]

Something very important underlies this 'playful' approach to culture: cultural consumption and engagement is productive. As an idea, culture is not like education or the NHS but learning and health. It is not 'delivered' by a single service but emerges from a complex set of interactions.

Cultural professionals must realise that they do not *deliver* culture; they build the encounters in which we *create* culture.

Visitors to Tate Britain pass a display stand. Leaflets on offer propose different tours we can take around the collections: so far, so conventional. Pick up one of the leaflets, and we realise that these are different from the tours we might have expected. They take their themes not from the canons of art history, but from us – our moods, our tempers, our feelings and our thoughts. We can take a 'first date' tour, an 'I've just split up' tour, or even an 'I'm hung over' tour.

The pamphlets balance professional curation and viewer response. For Nicholas Serota, Tate's director, the 'different modes and levels of interpretation . . . create a matrix of changing relationships to be explored by visitors according to their particular interests and sensibilities'.[6] This logic underlies the new cultural professionalism: its role is to create and engineer those modes and levels of interpretation and build from the individual's personal response.

In the Tate leaflets, the experts at the gallery use their skills to select works according to the moods that they know everyone shares. This is *not* dumbing down for mass appeal. It gives viewers a way to enter into conversation with work on their own terms. From this point, people are much more willing and confident to respond to the professional as a guide to some of the other meanings that the work might contain.

The final, blank leaflet on the stand is the most significant of all. It offers visitors the chance to compile their own tour. Working from principles shaped by their own experiences and opinions, viewers can share ways of engaging with the collections that bring new life and perspectives to a common cultural asset. By encouraging the participation of their public, and giving it a voice, cultural professionals find ways in which to engage the public and to help them create meaning.

Creating cultural value with other professionals

Engagement with culture thrives on personalised support from professionals, but the cultural sector struggles to sustain this kind of activity. Meanwhile cultural professionals themselves are demonstrating this kind of support and freedom, and its ability to foster cultural value.

The pressures on cultural professionals to attract more diverse visitors, the obligation to contribute to regional economies and the duty to contribute to instrumental agendas all mount up to be very time-consuming and capacity-hungry demands. Up and down the country, cultural professionals have proved that they are worth their salt in meeting them, but this can distract from the essence of what they do.

To overcome this pressure on capacity, Creative Partnerships collaborate with the education sector. In so doing, it is the work that cultural and creative professionals do – and not the targets that they hit – that is important.

This is especially the case in the work that Theatre Cap-a-Pie undertook with young people, aged only five, to script and direct their own play, *Mary Lou and the Ice Cream Pirates*. Supported by Creative Partnerships Durham Sunderland, the play is distinctive because the cultural professionals were the actors being directed. The play was subsequently put on in front of a paying audience at the company's theatre in Dipton, County Durham. As a result, it was imperative that the play would be both of a quality that would reflect their professionalism and an excellent learning experience for the young participants. To ensure this, they allowed the young people ownership of the play, giving them the means of developing a story that reflected their own experience and helping them learn to use culture as a means of expression.

Initially, the story began simply: it was the tale of two brothers, one good, the other bad. Soon, the young people realised that – for the plot to flow – the brothers could not have such fixed roles. Building from the experience of their own lives, they developed the characters so that one would be good at one time, bad at another, and that they would cooperate and fall out with equal variation. The cultural professionals worked with the young people to articulate their own perspective of the world around them.

However, their own professional need – putting on a commercially and professionally sustainable play – remained. On one solitary occasion, the professionals working on *Mary Lou* overrode the young people's decisions: from their expertise, they knew that the story needed a dénouement, and so they changed the script. The young people, however, rejected this: it did not chime with what they wanted. In one step, the play risked changing from being a means of expression to being an exercise. However, because the professionals had won their trust as experts, helping them to express themselves creatively, they could convince the young people of the need for change. The success of *Mary Lou* as a learning experience is demonstrated by the young people's determination to decide the nature of that change – they had successfully learned that the play was an expression of their own point of view, the very premise of engagement.

What mattered most for the young people and the actors alike was the integrity of the finished product. The professionals working on *Mary Lou* faced three demands: their status as professionals; the young people's status as authors and learning participants; and the public's interest as an audience. Crucially for the future of the cultural profession, the young people's learning experience grew out of the balance between these three demands. They were not directly accountable to any solely instrumental agenda, only the needs of those involved.[7]

Cultural professionals provide opportunities to create, and to use culture to bring our opinion to bear on the world. As a result, cultural professionals must be funded not as deliverers of a product, but as creators of value. This model is more suited to the new cultural professionalism because:

O   its guiding principle is the idea of value creation, rather than fulfilling fixed and pre-determined delivery
O   in educational terms, it helped young people to learn that cultural production and consumption is a way of engaging with others' opinions
O   its value is based on its integrity in relation to the participants
O   it is based on the particular cultural and creative skills that the professionals can bring and the potential in others that they can unlock
O   its success is judged primarily in terms that are cultural: payment by the audience to see a cultural product, the cultural creation of the young people and the learning that they derive, and the professional satisfaction of the practitioner.

Equal engagement

The Tate leaflets and *Mary Lou* are taken from very different aspects of our culture. This diversity is at the heart of the new cultural democracy: we have at our disposal a mass of vibrant and diverse opinion and expression. In today's Britain, cultural professionals have a more important role than ever before in helping to support this diversity.

Because culture is a means of accessing and understanding others' opinions, *different* cultural forms must be given the same voice that is given to different opinions in our society. Cultural professionals must equate these voices and give them expression. Widening engagement is not simply about introducing people to so-called 'high' culture. Cultural professionals should encourage and promote different forms of culture, using their skills to identify meaning in a range of cultural forms and relate this to a range of audiences from the public, through to politicians.

Theatre-goers on London's South Bank might walk by the groups of skateboarders that congregate there. However, as the crowds who gather to watch them recognise, the skaters are no more or no less engaging in a cultural form than the actors in the theatre alongside them. Too often, culture is distinguished from what is called 'counter-culture'. In policy, especially, where culture is gaining credibility, cultural professionals must use their expertise to draw out the values of all forms of culture, giving them an equal voice and representation in our cultural decisions. If skateboarding is something forever associated with the South Bank, might we one day see it represented on the Board of the Royal Festival Hall?

Some champions of counter-culture are already emerging. In the run-up to the 2006 Commonwealth Games, much of Melbourne's street art was painted over. The graffiti artist, Banksy, has described this as 'obliterating a unique and vibrant culture overnight',[8] and fears the same might happen in the preparation of London's Olympic Games in 2012. As he points out, opinion outside the cultural sector agrees. Alison Young, head of the Department of Criminology at Melbourne University, was commissioned by the city council to draw up a graffiti strategy – her response was to propose a tolerance zone, where the wilful expressions represented by the artists could go unpunished. Whether this would have worked or not, we do not know. The public supported the idea of a tolerance zone, but the council rejected it. 'The clean-up is an imposition of a supposedly mainstream, or dominant, cultural view,' said Young.[9]

It is telling that the city council turned to a criminologist for a solution to what it saw as the problem of graffiti. It reveals the false hierarchy of cultural forms that continues to pervade contemporary attitudes to culture. More than that, it is a case in point in which cultural professionals and the valuable expertise that they can provide can relate to issues conventionally seen as being beyond their remit. If more attention was paid to the culture that street art, free-skating and other so-called 'counter-cultural' forms represent, then we might well discover that aspects of our culture usually seen as problems might in fact be the reverse. In the run-up to the 2012 Olympic Games, and in other areas of policy, we must show greater sensitivity to various forms as a means of cultural expression. Cultural professionals and the expertise that they bring will be essential in doing so.

Conclusion

If we recognise the valuable engagement that cultural professionals can provide to the public, then we have to support them by implementing structures of support and funding that are more attuned to this goal. Broadly speaking, the problems are that:

O instrumental demands on the cultural professional often leaves the public out of the equation
O funding models often assume that cultural professionals operate at the behest of the government and in response to agendas external to the sector
O culture is often seen as something that is delivered rather than created
O there is a gap between the inherent and unique values that we all associate with culture and the ways in which cultural professionals are forced to articulate their role
O the rich media of expression that surround us are often ignored by a focus on what is conventionally seen as 'high culture'.

Only by understanding culture as a form of expression can we take steps towards the cultural democracy that the Minister for Culture rightly values. Cultural professionals must be recognised as the people who can help us to achieve this. Only when this is more generally understood and given credibility in policy and government circles will our cultural professionals be able to realise their full potential.

This requires that:

- O cultural professionals should be more assertive of their role in democratic contexts
- O cultural professionals should express the value of their activities in terms that speak equally to values that they identify in the cultural form, the values that the public place on it, and the existing instrumental aims of funders
- O funders and policy-makers should view culture as a means of expression and a good that should be enabled in its own right and not trammelled by instrumental agenda
- O means of engaging the public in cultural activity should be developed with a view to creating new meaning rather than simply attracting more numbers: that meaning should be recorded in ways that can be fed back to subsequent visitors and audiences
- O funding models should be restructured to support the creation of potential – funding bodies should take responsibility for instrumental functionality, mediating between policy requirements and the concerns of the public, and the cultural and creative professionals and so ensure that cultural activity is based on the relationship between expert and public
- O greater responsibility is given and more attention is paid to cultural professionals in general decisions in areas that range from health to local government: a cultural voice should be heard on every public board
- O a public voice should be heard on every cultural board, bringing the public into decision-making processes in the cultural realm
- O public cultural policy should engage with culture in the widest, democratic sense and not be limited to institutionalised categories: the expertise that cultural professionals have in understanding cultural forms should be used more effectively to understand different forms of cultural expression.

This is not a manifesto for reform. The different challenges that face the cultural profession at the turn of the twenty-first century, the different ways in which it has adapted to meet them and the suggestions for how it can develop further are intended to provoke discussion and further thought.

Culture is neither a force for good nor for bad: it is an expression of many opinions and attitudes, diverse in nature. If we are to understand them fully, and make the most of all the cultural interactions across our society, then cultural professionals are essential to our future.

Sam Jones is a researcher at Demos.

Notes

1   D Lammy, 'Cultural democracy', speech to Demos, 29 Mar 2006.
2   J Holden, *Cultural Value and the Crisis of Legitimacy* (London: Demos, 2006).
3   J Delingpole, 'What are museums for?', *The Times*, 17 Mar 2006.
4   M Moore, *Creating Public Value* (Cambridge, MA: Harvard University Press, 1997).
5   Ibid.
6   Quoted in N Prior, 'Having one's Tate and eating it', in A McClellan (ed), *Art and its Publics: Museum studies at the millennium* (Malden, MA: Blackwell Publishing, 2003).
7   The discussion of *Mary Lou* is based on the relationship between the professionals, the politicians and the public as identified by John Holden in *Cultural Value and the Crisis of Legitimacy*.
8   'The writing on the wall', *Guardian*, 24 Mar 2006 (the information on Melbourne's graffiti is taken from this article).
9   Ibid.

2. The activist police force

Charlie Edwards

There are restrictive practices that prevent police forces from delivering the kind of policing people want. We should be more aggressive in breaking down the barriers in the way of a professional, twenty-first-century police force, whether it's political correctness from above, or ploddishness from below.

David Cameron MP

When Richard Handford became the new executive producer of the ITV series *The Bill*, he set about changing the format of the series. Not content with changing the cast and story lines, Hanford decided to change *how* the police fought crime. No longer were cases solved in 25 minutes by police officers racing their squad cars around, kicking down doors and arresting would-be criminals. Instead plots spanned many episodes, and quite often a minor offence dealt with by uniformed police officers in one episode would re-appear a few weeks later as part of a major case for the CID. Handford's ideas were not just about creating 'cliff-hangers'; he wanted to reflect the true complexity of crime and policing. In the process, Handford portrayed a more progressive, responsive and citizen-focused police service.

The reality of policing has also shifted in this direction, but it has taken rather more work. It has required a process of cultural change which continues to this day, as the police service seeks to become more proactive and more sophisticated in serving the public. As then

Home Secretary Charles Clarke told a conference in January 2005: 'It must seem sometimes that there is a process of perpetual change but society is changing fast around us. We have to find the right way to change in order to meet those challenges. That's why the Citizen-Focused Policing relationship is central to everything we do.'[1] The key implication of this principle is a new – or renewed – focus on neighbourhood policing. The police reform white paper, *Building Communities, Beating Crime: A better police service for the 21st century* states:

> *The Government believes that, as a starting point, we need revitalised neighbourhood policing for today's world. Our clear view is that increasing public trust and confidence in policing – while important in its own right – will also be a real benefit for the police service itself. It will help make policing more effective.*[2]

This echoes an early report on modernising the police service by Her Majesty's Inspectorate of the Constabulary (HMIC) which suggested that:

> *The key challenge is to make the service more professional and to enrich the role and contribution of all staff in providing the best possible service to our communities. In doing so, whilst change will be inevitable, it is equally vital that we retain the core values inherent in the office and powers of a constable that have made policing in Britain the envy of police services across the world.*[3]

Within policing, the challenge of professionalisation is the challenge of building a culture of confidence and competence around the task of actively shaping our public realm. The fundamental task facing the police, in other words, is the transformation of their operational capacity.

Over the last two years, Demos has worked to guide groups of senior police officers through a 'futures thinking' exercise, imagining policing in 2020. The scenarios were originally developed by participants on the Strategic Command Course in December 2003 and these ideas have since been tested and refined by more than 150 officers.[4] The process has offered an invaluable opportunity to interrogate the future of police operations, and to garner the views of those who will shape it. Engaging with tomorrow's 'top cops' has been a hugely rewarding way to gather and test out ideas. It is the lessons of this work on which this essay is based, as well as the longer pamphlet *A Force for Change*.[5]

In response to Cameron's suggestion that the government 'should be more aggressive in breaking down the barriers in the way of a professional, twenty-first-century police force', the new head of the National Policing Improvement Agency (NPIA) argues that the police are very far from being 'the last great unreformed public service'. He points to the 'major review of the post-1962 police force structure', 'a significant investment in community support officers' and the new Serious and Organised Crime Agency (SOCA) as examples of how the police are adapting to the new challenges they face.

Our police forces are certainly changing fast. Government has shifted the role of policing to 'reassurance' through community-based policing, moved officers from desk-based jobs to the streets and introduced 'community support officers' (CSOs) to the police family. Alongside workforce reform, police officers are making much greater use of technology and work more and more in partnership with other agencies and with the public.

While this approach has been accepted by senior police officers, who have long complained of 'mission creep' and the lack of support they receive from government agencies, they have also caused some difficulties. However, more significant is the deep culture change of which they are a part. To succeed in the twenty-first century, today's police officers must learn to give up their monopoly over issues of law and order and grow into a more proactive and 'political' role in shaping the society around them.

Public value policing

When Robert Peel founded the police service in the nineteenth century, he finally won a long and bitter battle with opponents who said that such a move threatened the essential liberties of the British people.

The debate between Peel and his critics goes to the heart of questions about how we think about the value of our public services. Peel's critics argued that it was not in individuals' self-interest to give up their freedom, in the form of extra powers for the state and higher taxes, to support the creation of a police force. Maybe so, said Peel, but it was still in their *collective* interest to do so. As he is reported to have told Wellington, 'I want to teach people that liberty does not consist in having your house robbed by organised gangs of thieves, and in leaving the principal streets of London in the nightly possession of drunken women and vagabonds.'[6]

Today, the challenge of ensuring and demonstrating that the police are serving collective interests remains as crucial as ever. Indeed, it connects with important contemporary work on public services and public policy – the idea of 'public value'. Public value takes as its starting point the idea that leaders in public services cannot take the underlying purpose of their institution, its legitimacy, or the value it creates for citizens to be self-evident, simply because they are public institutions whose mandate has been supplied by democratically elected governments. Instead, the leaders of our public services need to focus on operational capacity, legitimacy and support, and values, mission and goals. It is the issue of organisational capacity on which we focus in this essay.

The operating challenge

The police face a growing number of competing demands. Today, the pressure of these demands is reaching a critical level. To respond, police officers will have to challenge deeply held beliefs about their own profession.

For example, public concern about prevalent anti-social and nuisance behaviour and its impact on quality of life grew during the 1990s, creating a demand for the police to focus on local issues and 'level 1' crime.[7] Although people perceive that specific types of behaviour have fallen from their peak a few years ago, their overall perception of anti-social behaviour is that it is still getting worse.[8] However, at the same time, the need for the police to tackle 'level 3' threats – terrorist networks, organised crime, drugs and people-trafficking – has been brought home vividly by a number of incidents over the last year, from the deaths of the Morecambe cocklers, illegal migrant workers killed by the negligence of their gangmaster, to the 52 men and women murdered in the 7 July bombings on the London transport system.

Is it feasible for the police to continue to cover such a wide terrain? Many within the service argue that it simply has to be feasible, because 'omni-competence' is integral to the values of the police service. Others claim that omni-competence is a dangerous and unsustainable fiction, and that more work should be hived off to other (and more specialised) agencies at every level, from local authorities at the neighbourhood level to SOCA at the national level.

The London bombings appear to lend weight to both camps. On the one hand, they have shown that in the age of the home-grown suicide bomber, effective national intelligence needs strong local roots into communities. On the other, the targeting of particular ethnic minorities makes cooperative, high-trust relationships with local communities (and particularly the British Muslim community) seem both more necessary and less feasible than ever.

This dilemma, therefore, cannot be resolved simply by focusing on what the police *do*. The police need to improve their ability to draw on work to which they are connected or with which they have a relationship. In doing so the police need to learn to shape explicit priorities on which they can focus and to allow other organisations and the public to help to achieve them. In other words, they need to be smarter at engaging in the political process at national and local levels and get better at creating and sustaining partnership.

The challenge in improving the police's partnership working is to address their reluctance to let other agencies take more of the strain. Since 1984, the police have been expected to operate through multiagency partnerships, particularly in the delivery of crime prevention activity.[9] The 'joining-up' agenda gathered pace after the election of the Labour government in 1997. Section 17 of the Crime and Disorder Act 1998 placed a duty on the local authority 'to exercise its various functions with due regard to the likely effect of the exercise of those functions on, and the need to do all it reasonably can to prevent crime and disorder in its area'. Crime and Disorder Reduction Partnerships (CDRPs), linking the police to local authorities, other statutory agencies, the private sector and community and voluntary groups, are now an important focus for policing activities.

But many Basic Command Unit (BCU) commanders are sceptical about CDRPs, suggesting that they are little more than talking shops unless the police really take responsibility for driving them forward. Some senior officers profess concern that the police's 'can-do attitude', an asset in so many operational settings, is actually damaging for long-term strategy. It breeds a 'mission creep', often not formally recognised or accompanied by additional resources, leaving the police's operational capacity spread ever more thinly across an expanding range of priorities, and clarity about the core purposes of policing is lost. Other officers believe the police themselves must share some of the responsibility for their reluctance to trust other agencies and refusal to compromise any of their operational independence, even if ultimately it would increase the capability to get the job done. Finally, some officers believe that the only way forward is to create 'local accountability frameworks' that allow the public to see which agencies are involved at any one time. In the words of one senior officer: 'We bring it [overstretch] on ourselves. . . . We don't trust anyone else to do anything but us.' For another: 'If what really matters is fear of crime and reassurance, and that agenda is too broad for us to manage by ourselves, we need to work in partnership and be evaluated as such.'

Alongside the need to improve their partnership working, senior police officers need to improve the ways in which they engage with politics. However, this rubs up against professional values forged in times of strife, which see political engagement as only one step removed from political interference. Concerns about political interference re-emerged on the national scene in the 1980s. The Thatcher government's mass mobilisation of the police service in its conflict with the National Union of Mineworkers during the Miners' Strike was hugely divisive, particularly in the northern areas most affected by the strike. Many viewed it as politicisation, with the police becoming an arm of the state rather than a servant of the law. For a number of serving senior police officers today, the Miners' Strike was a key formative moment in their early careers that entrenched a deep hostility to political interference.

An activist police force

As a result, a key issue for police professionals is the trust and confidence they have in working with other organisations and in working *in public*. Difficult as it is, this is an important challenge for police officers to face as a profession as circumstances continue to change.

As we have seen, for some police officers, the introduction of CSOs has been a cause for anxiety. However, arguably it is only the tip of the iceberg. A number of actors from the wider 'policing family' are beginning to encroach on traditional police turf. Security companies, voluntary organisations and local authorities increasingly provide reassurance services such as neighbourhood wardens. Specialist services such as forensics, divers, helicopters, the management of custody suites, cyber-crime and other high-value investigation services are or could soon be offered by private providers. As the operating environment changes, the question is what role police will play as quality assurers, brokers, commissioners and coordinators in this more diverse market.

Naturally, the police profession will want to be at the heart of decisions of this kind. However, in order that they can be, they must make two important shifts. First, there must be greater collaboration between forces with different specialisms, and the police force must embrace a role for a more diverse range of providers of policing services – including the private sector – where it brings benefits. Indeed, police leaders should make clear their commitment to partnership working by building on the best practices of existing arrangements. They should push for coterminous boundaries with other partners, pooled budgets, common targets and accountability frameworks, and a shared leadership under a 'director of community safety', who might be a police officer or from another agency. The capacity of policing to create public value is greater than the capacity of the police to create public value. Rather than resist the growth of the 'policing family', the police should harness and shape it.

Second, while independence is a non-negotiable for the police, it cannot be at the expense of 'splendid isolation'. Impartiality cannot mean the police always know best. Although reticence in forging connections to local local politics is understandable, this must form an approach to engagement rather than legitimise a police monopoly over law and order. Public engagement needs to be expressed in practical relationships between the police and the community, not abstract structures. Done properly, community participation can help solve problems for police officers; it need not be seen simply as a way of causing them.

Whatever happens over the next 15 years, policing as a profession cannot stand still. Its work must become more open and better connected to those the police serve. From the growth of para-professional support to the rise of more specialist roles to demands for greater accountability from communities and politicians, the traditional bases on which policing bound itself together and claimed legitimacy are being undermined. Rather than resist these pressures, police officers should embrace change as an opportunity to renew policing as what Judyth Sachs calls an 'activist profession':

> An activist profession is one that is open to ideas and influence from the communities it serves, actively seeks to build trust with those communities, has a clear vision of the society it is trying to create in the future, and which recognises the importance of engaging in political forums to help realise that future. Such a culture exists in pockets of the police service, but it is far from widespread.[10]

Charlie Edwards is a researcher at Demos.

Notes

1 Citizen-Focused Policing, conference, London, Jan 2005; cited in C Edwards and P Skidmore, *A Force For Change: Policing 2020* (London: Demos, 2006), see www.demos.co.uk/catalogue/aforceforchange (accessed 24 May 2006).
2 Home Office, *Building Communities, Beating Crime: A better police service for the 21st century*, police reform white paper (London: Home Office, 2004).
3 Her Majesty's Inspectorate of the Constabulary, 'Modernising the Police Service', HMIC thematic report, January 2004.
4 These officers all took part in the 'Policing contexts and futures' module of the Senior Leadership Development Programme II run by Centrex, the police training and development organisation.
5 Edwards and Skidmore, *A Force for Change* (London: Demos, 2006).
6 See www.historyhome.co.uk/peel/laworder/police.htm (accessed 24 May 2006).
7 Levels 1, 2 and 3 refer to the National Intelligence Model (NIM). The NIM was designed by the National Criminal Intelligence Service (NCIS) in 2000 to professionalise the intelligence discipline within law enforcement by planning and working in cooperation with partners to secure community safety, to manage performance and risk, and to account for budgets.
8 M Wood, *Perceptions and Experience of Antisocial Behaviour: Findings from the 2003/2004 British Crime Survey*; see www.homeoffice.gov.uk/rds/pdfs04/rdsolr4904.pdf (accessed 24 May 2006).
9 Home Office, *Crime Prevention, interdepartmental circular 8/84* (London: Home Office, 1984), cited in J Bright, *Turning the Tide* (London: Demos, 1997).
10 See S Groundwater Smith and J Sachs, 'The activist professional and the reinstatement of trust'; available at www.acij.uts.edu.au/archives/profprac/activist.pdf (accessed 24 May 2006).

3. The career planning professional

John Craig

Gillian began working for the careers service in her early twenties, in a tightly defined administrative role – 'I used to have to ask for permission to send out a letter,' she says. Today, working as an Activate adviser with groups of teenagers, Gillian's career is developing fast. Asked about the changes Careers Scotland has brought, she points to the variety of her work: 'There is more scope, more opportunity, a chance to develop yourself if you want to,' she says. And for Gillian, this has enabled her to make a significant transition. 'In terms of a professional, you tend to think of someone with a university degree, but I feel like I am a professional too. I've become a professional.'

Wendy, in contrast, is this classical kind of professional. Wendy applied to become a careers adviser ten years ago, before there was a Scotland-wide structure to the profession. She didn't like the idea of a 'lack of national clout' and pulled out, becoming a lawyer instead. However, since the creation of Careers Scotland, Wendy has made the switch from law to join the organisation.

Today, Wendy and Gillian work side by side as members of the Parkhead centre in Glasgow, and for them their professionalism lies in their commitment to their clients and to each other.

Life for professionals at Careers Scotland is changing fast, as these two examples show. In response to changing economic circumstances, the organisation is looking to improve the quality of the advice its professionals give and to use professional regulation to drive this improvement. In the process, we are arguably witnessing a professionalisation of career planning. However, in return, we are also seeing a new settlement development between Careers Scotland and the professionals on which it relies. In both these senses, there is a growing equivalence between the professionalism of staff at Careers Scotland and that of lawyers, accountants and management consultants.[1]

As professions come under pressure to innovate and to demonstrate that they are working in the public interest, Careers Scotland is embracing change. The organisation is building a profession that is at once more open – to change and to newcomers – more autonomous and more effective. This is a complex task, involving deep change to the work of career planning professionals and to the ways in which they and the public understand their role.

As it pursues change, Careers Scotland is learning lessons that will strike a chord with professionals across the public and private sectors. Career planning professionals are rapidly coming to terms with the idea that to be a professional is to practise in public and to acknowledge collective responsibility. They are beginning to model a professionalism based not on exclusivity and status but on negotiation with the public, showing in the process that their own autonomy and that of their clients can grow together. Career planning professionals serve as an important example of a new settlement between organisational and professional life, which is of growing significance to professionalism in every sphere.

Changes at Careers Scotland

Changes at Careers Scotland reflect changes in the Scottish economy. As individuals take greater responsibility for their own careers,[2] the kind of career planning that was once the preserve of the ambitious few has become a universally important life skill. Today, the research tells us that 'most employees . . . are constantly on the lookout for alternative opportunities'.[3] To take control of our career, rather than become a cork on the tide of our local labour market, we must all develop these skills.

The rise of the knowledge economy and decline of Scotland's manufacturing sector mean that fewer jobs await those with few qualifications and career plans. Increasingly, this is as much a story of technology replacing jobs as it is technology enabling them to be outsourced. As Richard Sennett points out, as technology creates new jobs it also destroys others.[4] While manufacturing output in Scotland, for example, has declined by 12 per cent since 1999,[5] across the UK the proportion of the labour force working in manufacturing has declined by double that amount.[6] To find work, growing numbers have to demonstrate that they can do work that machines *cannot* do.

As the skills of employees become more important, so their effect on people's pay is becoming more significant. Across Europe, the changing nature of work is increasingly driving a 'wedge between unemployment risks of the least qualified school leavers and those with more advanced levels of education'.[7] The ability to tread a path through which one's skills and contacts can develop, therefore, is vital to one's quality of life, and this is increasingly recognised by governments across the developed world.[8]

It is these challenges to which Careers Scotland is seeking to respond. Careers Scotland has begun with a recognition that the shifts that make education and training more vital and economies more volatile also have the potential to empower individuals. As in many leading careers services internationally, the focus is shifting towards encouraging clients to answer their own questions – to self-help.[9] From improved transport to a helpline and the internet, people can access a wider range of jobs and information for themselves.

In re-designing its approach, Careers Scotland has sought to exploit the potential of these structural changes. The effect of this is twofold: Careers Scotland is working to meet expectations of a personalised service and to challenge expectations of ready-made solutions to questions about careers.

To meet expectations of a personalised service, Careers Scotland has expanded substantially its use of the telephone and the internet. Where in the past clients simply made appointments to see an adviser, today people use the service *when* they want, *where* they want, in the *way* they want. In addition, they have invested in television adverts, raising the profile of career planning and explaining to the public what they can expect from the service. Building on this new visibility, Careers Scotland has embarked on an ambitious capital investment programme, rationalising the number of centres but investing in highly visible and accessible shop front premises. These new centres model the practice of dropping in to Careers Scotland at a moment convenient to the client rather than the professional.

The imperative of personalisation has also demanded that Careers Scotland become much more effective and systematic in assessing and responding to individual needs. As a result, the organisation has worked to establish a range of shared national practices where once there was considerable variation. Clear national models now structure the 'career planning journey', which advisers take clients through, and crucially the operating model has helped to create a shared approach to differentiating support, sorting clients between one of three levels of engagement: 77 per cent of clients are allocated to self-help services, 19 per cent to assisted services and 4 per cent receive in-depth services. In turn, this helps Careers Scotland to achieve a vital objective: the focus of its resources where they are most needed.

However, in the creation of a seamless service, they are nevertheless looking for new ways to animate clients as active participants in career planning, rather than as passive recipients of advice. In learning to balance the demands of serving and animating its clients, Careers Scotland is now in an ongoing process of research and development, refining national practice. It is working to create an organisation in which all staff can clearly see and help to shape national best practice and where this best practice reaches all staff.

Professional angst and opportunity

Our purpose here is not to evaluate the changes wholesale but to understand their significance for career planning professionals. As professional roles and public understanding of their work change, staff have responded in a range of ways. Naturally, for some, such rapid change has brought insecurity about professionalism. Across professional work in the UK, the idea that 'you are what you do' is gaining currency, so that professional change can be personally threatening. As one respondent commented: 'Anything that's suggested, good, bad or indifferent, the answer is no . . . "because I'm a professional, this is the only way I can do it".'

Careers planning professionals themselves are clear that in recent years their ability to thrive has depended heavily on their confidence, resilience and entrepreneurship. Those employees who have depended more heavily on structure and routine have found the changes at Careers Scotland more difficult to absorb. Analysis of our research interviews suggests that these people tend to be those who are in their mid-forties or older *and* have been in career planning since before the inception of Careers Scotland in 2002.

In interviews, this group exhibited signs of professional conservatism. There were suggestions that the role of careers advisers be more tightly restricted to those with particular training, theoretical knowledge and understanding of the history of the discipline. Interviewees were concerned about the relative status of careers planning compared with other professions. Finally, there was some anxiety that in the focus on client self-help the public might get the impression that career planning is merely 'common sense'.

However, for everyone we spoke to in this group, we found an equal number of enthusiastic early adopters of changes in Careers Scotland. Many members of staff appreciated the space for creativity that change had opened up, and were working to sketch out a new role for the profession. Two key elements of this new role can help to explain this range of responses and point towards their resolution.

Growing autonomy together

For careers advisers, one phenomenon sums up the new world in which they operate – the internet. Professional knowledge about opportunities and labour market dynamics, which once very difficult to generate and spread, is now openly available. Career planning professionals are having to show that their professionalism is about much more than the information they hold, because increasingly that information is everywhere. As Isabelle, a careers adviser for over 20 years, points out: 'In the past, our professionalism came from our knowledge . . . because clients couldn't get access to the information . . . today information is so accessible.'

In the past, professions have used accredited knowledge to police professional boundaries, ensuring control of a given practice. The information revolution means that today this is much harder to do. Where once professional control was a matter of necessity, therefore, today it has to be earned – professionals have to demonstrate that they add value in the public interest.

Doctors, for example, demonstrate added value very successfully. They increasingly find patients arriving for consultations with reams of internet printout, clear that they have diagnosed their condition and selected a prescription. However, for the public, doctors retain a key role that is about much more than their expertise. Doctors' experience, communication skills and ethical standards mean that the public is very happy for them to take ongoing responsibility for our health. Careers advisers must achieve the same.

As expertise that was once the preserve of a profession spreads, it can be an uncertain, stressful experience. While the comparison with doctors is a heartening one, we might also make a comparison with travel agents. For travel agents, tools like Google have been bad news. The tasks of working out what holidays might suit people, how to put them together and who to buy them from have effectively been automated. Travel agents' advice, judgement and expertise have been marginalised.

Some professional anxiety about demonstrating added value, therefore, is natural. For one careers adviser, for example, Google was 'not a bad thing . . . but that kind of proliferation can make things very confusing for the client'. For another, there was frustration that an emphasis on self-help challenged the public perception of careers advisers as helpful and supportive. On telling a young man that the service no longer distributed lists of employers, his mother replied: 'Oh, you're not as helpful as you were with my eldest son.' The question from professionals, in effect, was: why show people how to use a map when you could just point them to where they are going? Underlying this question seemed to be anxiety about a profession saying publicly that it does *not* have all the answers.

However, for Careers Scotland, this is a hugely important step. Andrew Paine, a careers planning executive, remembers: 'In the old model, it was as if careers advisers were supposed to have some seer quality – mystical insight into job options and personal destinies . . . and as careers advisers, we were going along with that.' This seer quality returns again and again in the way advisers themselves describe their public image. Even today, advisers feel variously that the public see them as 'mind-readers' and 'magicians', even their own personal 'Mystic Meg'. While this perception bolsters the status of career planning professionals, it can actually undermine their effectiveness.

For senior staff at Careers Scotland, career planning professionals have for too long given in to the temptation of accepting the kudos that this magical status inevitably brings. As Isabelle found when her client's mother accused her of being unhelpful, the kind of reliance this model creates can be a comfortable place to be and a difficult one to break out of. However, in changed economic circumstances, it is no longer the best way to serve the public.

As career planning professionals find the confidence to step away from their seer image, they are beginning to add the kind of value we expect from professionals. As Kate Hasson, also a careers planning executive, puts it: at their best those in career planning are 'supporting clients to become equal partners'. For example, Wendy and Gillian with whom we began say they have learnt that they can no longer survive as careers advisers by pretending to know everything. 'Maybe the person in front of you will become a pilot,' says Gillian, or perhaps you are in an interview with the next platinum-selling popstar. Instead of a *transactional* model in which staff dispense advice and information, this enables *transformational* work. By conceding that they do not have all they answers, career planning professionals can look with clients not only at the employment environment around them but also at their own assumptions, ambitions and skills, building their capacity and confidence to plan their career.

In this way, careers advisers are increasingly discovering that, in some circumstances, the more power you give away, the more power you have – they are helping both professional and client to achieve more. Like other professionals today, they are discovering that their autonomy and that of their clients can grow together. As another careers adviser put it: 'We have to be happy that our professionalism is based on something other than our professional knowledge . . . theoretical understanding underpinning models of guidance . . . cover planning and the process to go through to reach an effective decision.'

However, in negotiating new autonomy with their clients, career planning professionals are aware that they are also opening themselves up to new sources of challenge and critique. As one put it: 'Our work is far less tangible now . . . with Careers Scotland, and possibly education, everyone can put in their two-pence worth.' Careers Scotland is helping its staff to build the kind of confidence and resilience that can see this openness become a strength rather than a weakness. In the process, at its best at least, this public challenge is being translated into a force for innovation rather than an obstacle for professionals.

The politics of professionalism

Career planning professionals are not simply doing more professional work, they are also relying more heavily on professional norms and professional legitimacy. However, as they do so, the shape of their profession is changing. Where once career planning was a profession defined and regulated by individuals and accrediting universities, today large organisations like Careers Scotland are themselves playing a more important, proactive role.

As Careers Scotland has sought to improve services across the organisation, it has naturally sought to generate shared national approaches and models of best practice. Andrew Paine noted: 'In the early focus groups, we asked people, "what's your approach to career planning?" and people just laughed.' They weren't used to that kind of question; people simply 'cherry-picked' practice that appealed to them from different models and colleagues. As a result, the concern was that Careers Scotland was not giving a sufficient quantity of people a service of sufficient quality.

In response, Careers Scotland has played a much more active role in seeking to define what counts as a good career planning professional. As we have seen, it has developed national approaches to assessment and the 'career planning journey', working with university researchers. In addition it has developed new national modules of professional development and now funds staff membership of professional organisations.

As a result, there are two key ways in which career planning increasingly relies on professional regulation. First, norms of professional practice are much more highly codified than they have been in the past. In order for integrated national services to fit together, staff must be very disciplined – they must internalise a set of professional norms about exactly *how* they conduct their work. For some staff, this was difficult as they were 'used to being left alone'. Older staff 'miss the flexibility – the chance to do a wee bit of what they want to'. As one put it: 'I used to enjoy my time with clients; now it's all very target-driven.' Like so many professionals, beyond pay and duty, it is important to careers advisers to express themselves, intellectually and emotionally, through their work. In the past, this expression could happen individually – today career planning professionals must express themselves as part of a team.

The second way in which Careers Scotland relies increasingly on professional norms is in helping its staff to make more significant, potentially more controversial decisions. Today, careers planning professionals pay much closer attention to labour market intelligence – as one adviser put it: their work is no longer 'guidance in a vacuum'. As a result, more experienced members of staff were aware that they are now 'managing expectations much more consciously'. Where in the past, for example, an idealist career planner might have felt justified in allowing demand for apprenticeships to exceed supply, today they must help to match the two.

Rationing scarce resources in this way is a delicate and potentially controversial aspect of Careers Scotland's work. To ensure the legitimacy of these decisions, and staff confidence in making them, it needs to be connected to clear, public rationales and to be clearly accountable. Again, for some, this kind of collective responsibility was a stressful shift. A minority expressed the view that they were 'a careers adviser not a social worker' – that in this sense their professionalism was being 'blurred' and their responsibilities over-loaded. However, others seemed to relish this fuller professional role.

In this context, therefore, Careers Scotland's work looks very like a professionalisation of career planning. Its staff build the capacity of clients to plan their own careers, exhibit high-quality professional practice and make difficult decisions to manage scarce resources. However, to achieve this professionalisation, Careers Scotland has developed a new settlement with the profession, in which Careers Scotland itself has become much more significant as a site of professional regulation, development and debate. For staff, this is expressed as the sense that 'things are becoming politicised', that professionals are simply 'ticking a box' and being subjected to 'change for change's sake'.

Careers Scotland has sought to respond to these concerns to ensure that this new professional settlement is sustainable. While career planning professionals must take greater collective responsibility in their work, today they have much greater opportunity to shape both the work of their own teams and services and the national work of the organisation as a whole. There are new spaces in which career planning professionals can express themselves and be creative, but these spaces are very much within Careers Scotland.

Locally, as advisers engage in a broader range of activities and look to work more collaboratively with other services, there is much more space for entrepreneurship. In this sense, local services have much greater autonomy than ever before. Indeed, a number of the careers advisers we spoke to were engaged in research or pilot projects, or had taken on a particular organisational responsibility. In addition, new professional development work on reflective practice has created opportunities for advisers to 'talk together about what they do'.

Nationally, Careers Scotland has created 'priority boards', which aim to draw innovative ideas from across the system. These boards are today being re-modelled around the cross-cutting priorities of the organisation and opened up to include staff from across the country. Indeed, any member of staff now has the right to feed ideas into their work online, and the hope is that this will spark new professional relationships and create a demand for research and development funding at all levels of Careers Scotland.

For those at the heart of Careers Scotland, these changes are beginning to bear fruit. In Parkhead, where Gillian and Wendy are based, the team typifies a new culture of collective responsibility and commitment. For them, professionalism lies in a commitment to an ever-improving public service and in a commitment to each other. They have come to terms with the idea that today's professionals have to practise in public, their work justified in the language of democratic politics.

Conclusion

Staff at Careers Scotland are moving through a process of professional renewal, which for some has been a real challenge. Where in the past their professional status seemed to be set in stone, today it is clear that those in career planning must earn their professional status. Public trust and gratitude is harder to earn today than ever before but Careers Scotland has been working to secure it.

First, the work of career planners has become more professional. They are increasingly finding ways to enable their own autonomy and effectiveness and that of their clients to grow together. By opening up information about career planning, building people's skills and working to make them equal partners, both clients and professionals are benefiting.

Second, the work of Careers Scotland relies increasingly on professional regulation. Careers planning professionals are finding that political responsibility is increasingly inescapable. However, by strengthening their commitments to one another and to the public, they are ensuring that they can handle controversial issues in legitimate ways. They are also coming to terms with the reality that today to be a professional is to practise in public – to work collectively and accountably. Professional norms increasingly ensure the quality of career planners' work and serve to legitimise the difficult decisions they face.

In sum, therefore, one perspective on the changes at Careers Scotland is that of professionalisation. However, this may be a point of real debate with Careers Scotland staff. Professionalisation has come as part of a new settlement between professionals and the organisation for which they work. As part of its growth, Careers Scotland has moved into the sphere of the profession, as a space for professional dialogue and as a regulator in its own right. As a result, for career planning professionals, professional debate is increasingly organisational debate.

In this sense, the organisational structures of Careers Scotland arguably mimic traditional professional structures. This is of real significance for the public sector because it picks up on the most important professional trend in the private sector. As professions such as law, accountancy and consultancy move from partnership governance models to corporate models, their organisations too are placing greater emphasis on professional culture and the *ethos* of partnership. It is this benchmark that is the most significant one for Careers Scotland as it embarks on further reform.

Crucially, as these changes have progressed, Careers Scotland has had to help people think through: 'What's my place here? Where do I fit in?' Our interviews and focus groups with careers advisers show that, far from an optional extra, this has been vital to the process of helping the profession to evolve. It demonstrates the potential of allying professional reform to organisational reform and the ongoing power of ideas of professionalism to regulate services in the public interest.

Notes

1   See essays in this collection by Empson and by Kipping, Kirkpatrick and Muzio.
2   Y Baruch, 'Transforming careers: from linear to multidirectional career paths', *Career Development International* 9, no 1 (2004).
3   R Mano-Negrin, 'Job search modes and turnover', *Career Development International* 9, no 4/5 (2004).
4   R Sennett, *The Culture of the New Capitalism* (London: Yale University Press, 2006).
5   Scottish Chambers of Commerce, *Economic Overview*, 2006, see www.scottish-enterprise.com/publications/scotland-competing-with-the-world.pdf (accessed 25 May 2006).
6   Office of National Statistics, *Labour Force Survey: Historical quarterly supplement, table 22*, 2006, see www.statistics.gov.uk/STATBASE/ssdataset.asp?vlnk=7922 (accessed 25 May 2006).
7   M Gangl, 'Changing labour markets and early career outcomes: labour market entry in Europe over the past decade', *Work, Employment and Society* 16, no 1 (2002).
8   AG Watts, 'Career guidance policy: an international review', *Career Development Quarterly* 54, no 1 (2005).
9   Ibid.

4. The lead professional in children's services

Estelle Morris and Keith Brumfitt

The role of the lead professional – coordinating the work of others on a client's behalf – challenges both professional tribalism and the authority of professional expertise. However, it draws on something deeper: the ethical commitment to their clients that all children's services professionals share. The challenge for these professionals is to take this opportunity of working together in teams to re-shape professional habits around the needs of every child. To do so, they will need to learn to influence both their colleagues and their employers.

New authority in children's services

The creation of lead professionals is part of a much broader workforce reform agenda. At its best, public service reform seeks to 'overcome the limitations of paternalism and consumerism' by organising the work of skilled professionals around the real lives of individuals.[1] As David Miliband has argued, this promises both to bring out the best in public service staff and to bring a smile to those they serve. It is the challenge of creating personalised services of universally high quality.

In an effort to meet this challenge, *Every Child Matters* emphasises the professional responsibility to collaborate.[2] Staff whose focus has been education provision, children's health services, early years, social care and social work, youth work or youth justice are now expected to work extensively across professional groups as well as maintain and strengthen their expertise in their specialist area.

The creation of lead professionals arises from the government's belief that individuals and organisations working with children and young people, for all their efforts to place children at the centre of their work, could do more to integrate their activities. With different approaches to assessment and coordination across children's services, a small minority of children, young people and their families have experienced confusion and frustration. In recent years, a handful of very serious failures of the system were highlighted in child death inquiries, which gave new impetus to improvement efforts across children's services.

Lead professionals follow other work to enable staff to function as brokers on behalf of service users. In the 1990s, care management was introduced in adult social care and the 'key worker' concept to children's services. Where these models work well they have provided a high-quality, well-coordinated service, with straightforward lines of communication to and from the service user.

However, children's services continue to strive for further improvements. Occasionally, care managers are seen as remote, with little direct contact with or personal knowledge of service users. At the other end of the spectrum, key workers ensure that an individual child or young person is not overlooked and provides them with a first point of contact. They work with a child in a single setting, without an overview of the full range of services a child, young person or family receives. In contrast, lead professionals will work across a range of services *and* have much more direct day-to-day contact with children. As a result, the responsibilities and expectations of lead professionals are greater.

The lead professional role will be performed by those best placed to coordinate services on behalf of an individual child or young person. Consequently staff with a range of professional backgrounds will undertake the role. In many cases, their task will be to challenge the relatively isolated roles of those who work with children, listening as they do so to the concerns and ideas of their colleagues. To do this effectively, lead professionals will have to draw on resources that cut across professional backgrounds.

First, lead professionals will have to use skills and approaches common to all those working on behalf of children and young people, including effective communication, an ability to be assertive on behalf of a client or service user, good organisational skills, the ability to negotiate and liaise with others, and an ability to deliver required outcomes on time.

Second, like other professional groups, lead professionals will need to take an ethical stance on a range of issues, and demonstrate a set of values that others recognise as important. Although a set of values has not yet been agreed for those who work across all children's services, they are likely to include the rights of the child and, in particular, the right to be consulted on decisions that affect them. This is certainly implicit in practice across children's services. As a shared ethic for children's services professionals, this will be of crucial importance.

For example, decisions about who is best placed to take on the new role are important. If we accept that children and young people should be involved in decisions that affect them (a government requirement), they need to have a say in selecting their lead professional. However, those they prefer may not always be those with the necessary experience, skills, status, authority and capacity to undertake the role. How best to decide what is more important in identifying the lead professional – the person who appears to have the right skills and capacity or the one the child or young person wants if that person doesn't meet the first criteria – will be really important. How these decisions are made will offer an insight into the importance of the child's voice. Most importantly, they will create a lead professional role whose authority rests on representation of a client as well as expertise about what is best for them. To accommodate and work with this new source of authority, children's services professionals will need to emphasise shared ethical commitments to children over divergent expertise.

Open to dialogue and change

The success of the role of the lead professional will depend on the openness to new ideas of staff at all levels. For their part, children's services professionals will need to be willing to engage in new kinds of conversations about children and young people and work in new kinds of teams. Equally, policy-makers and managers will have to find innovative ways to free up lead professionals and to enable them to perform in their new role.

Because lead professionals are unlikely to know about every aspect of work with children and young people, they will need to consult those with specialist expertise. As it is for other professionals, the skill with which they engage in and broker these professional conversations will be vital. Indeed, at times it will need to be handled with particular diplomacy.

In addition to accessing specialist knowledge, lead professionals will require a range of other skills. They will need to collate and analyse large amounts of information to make informed judgements. They must be able to lead a new type of multidisciplinary team that is brought together to focus on the needs of a particular child, young person or family. Encouragingly, lead professionals are already building a body of knowledge about the best ways to meet these many demands and, through e-discussion groups hosted by the Children's Workforce Development Council, they are already sharing this knowledge with one another.

To work effectively across traditional professional boundaries requires patience, negotiating skills and an ability to be assertive in securing better outcomes for children or young people. Lead professionals will need to identify and engage with many other people to build a common understanding of a particular case and of the programme of services that they require. To achieve all this, the lead professional must be engaging, confident and assertive if bureaucracy is getting in the way or if resources are not being released or channelled effectively.

While all staff working in children's services will need to

understand how services are being reorganised, it is unrealistic for all of them to be trained as lead professionals. In practice many who undertake the role, will have to learn on the job. Amid colleagues of greater professional status, this may be a daunting task. While written guidance is available, by itself it may be insufficient. Additional web-based guidance with examples of effective practice, and locally based mentors who have already undertaken this role, would help to build the confidence of new staff and strengthen the skills and knowledge of serving lead professionals.

As more support is available, more professionals will take on the lead professional role. However, this will happen only when their other responsibilities change. Despite the strength of professionals' commitment to children's services, we know that people cannot accept additional work and responsibility without recompense in other areas. Lead professionals' managers have the ability to kick-start this initiative, yet they may not know how best to support their staff to undertake this new role. Without their help, their encouragement and their ability to re-assign other tasks, this new professional role may be stymied and fail to develop. External funding that covers staff time and provides space for training can support senior managers who intend to promote the lead professional role and make it happen.

A challenge for the whole system

Lead professionals will play a crucial role at the heart of our systems of children's services. They must help to develop shared approaches across the teams they lead and re-shape the attitudes of the agencies for which they work.

As the role of the lead professional becomes embedded, the next step is for lead professionals to take responsibility for managing the resources that have been assigned to an individual child or young person. As well as coordinating their services and providing a first point of contact for them, some professionals are being asked to be budget holders and managers. This means that a range of organisations will be asked to assign 'their' resources to the lead professional. For this to work, organisations will have to learn to live with the loss of direct control that this involves and lead professionals will have to demonstrate considerable tact and negotiation skills.

Ultimately, therefore, lead professionals bring greater freedom and responsibility to the teams of staff they coordinate for improving outcomes for children. Lead professionals must act as budget-holders in the interests of the child rather than those of particular services or institutions. This shows the extent to which lead professionals will play a crucial role both in shaping the team cultures in which this freedom can be exercised effectively and in changing the attitudes of those in the agencies around them.

Early signs in this regard are good, particularly where children and young people are kept at the centre of activities and the lead professional is properly resourced and supported. Further conditions for success will be identified through the evaluation of the pilot schemes for budget-holding lead professionals. But, however good the early signs are and even given a willingness to change, there is no room for complacency in the task of re-shaping professional roles. We should recognise that professionals need to be supported and prepared for any new role, provided with adequate resources and encouraged to promote the role to other staff who may be reluctant or unable to change. If we can avoid the syndrome of 'leave it to X – after all they are the lead professional', a great deal can be achieved. However, success in this endeavour will spiral, and it is crucial that we find ways to celebrate inter-professionalism where it helps children to receive better coordinated and more effective support and guidance. It is this success that will encourage more people to become lead professionals.

Children and young people who have complex needs or are at risk can be among the most vulnerable people in society. Lead professionals are not a pilot project – they are at the heart of our work to provide this group of children with the support they need. As a result, all those working with children and young people need to play their part in this team-based approach. A professional approach that values and supports the lead professional will contribute to positive outcomes for children and young people and help to grow the lead professional concept.

While this is a new professional role, it is based on a traditional view of recognising and valuing expertise wherever it is found. Importantly it acknowledges that when they collaborate, a team of diverse professionals can be greater than the sum of their parts. Lead professionals can be vital change agents in ensuring that this happens. We hope that the idea takes off and that over the next five years more staff will be freed from organisational hierarchies to work together to meet the needs of individual children.

Estelle Morris is Chair and Keith Brumfitt is Director of Research and Development at the Children's Workforce Development Council.

Notes

1   D Miliband, 'Foreword' in C Leadbeater, *Personalisation through Participation: A new script for public services* (London: Demos, 2004).

2   HM Government, *Every Child Matters: Change for children* (HM Government, 2004), see www.everychildmatters.gov.uk/_files/F9E3F941DC8D4580539EE4C743E9371 D.pdf (accessed 22 May 2006).

5. The plan is dead; long live the planner

Peter Bradwell and Inderpaul Johar

The key problem is no longer to ensure that our social and national systems are stable, it is to ensure that our . . . procedures are more adaptive.

Stephen Toulmin[1]

It is easy to speak of the democratic imperative to engage communities in the planning of their local environments. Development isn't simply the process of drawing a map; it impacts on the relationships between people, places, communities and the future they generate. But the complex nature of communities and their demands for autonomy make planning – and the role of the planner – increasingly problematic.

It is increasingly difficult for planning to reconcile local and national pressures. On one hand, as the principles of participation and local empowerment grow in popularity, it is easier for neighbourhoods to express their own views about their future. For example, planning legislation from 2004[2] builds in flexibility and the potential for greater community involvement in planning; the government's 'double devolution' agenda looks at shifting power not just to local authorities but to communities themselves; and Sir Michael Lyons's report[3] into local governance stresses the importance of locally led 'place-shaping'. On the other hand, national and global planning pressures, such as the need to increase dwelling density and reduce environment damage, are at least as strong as ever.

With the rise of localism, developing a planning narrative has become increasingly difficult because planning professionals have lost some of their traditional organisational power to the citizens they serve. As a result, they need to re-think traditional plan-led decision-making and recast their relationships with citizens and other stakeholders. When the plan is dead, what is the role of the planner?

Dispersed knowledge and the professional

Professional know-how is increasingly rivalled by that of their clients. Unprecedented access and availability of technical and factual information enabled by the internet has democratised knowledge, undermining exclusive professional power. This is as true for planners as it is for doctors. Today, savvy campaigners are challenging planning decisions armed with knowledge of legislation and technical processes.

At the same time, it is hard for planning officials to get a sense of how a neighbourhood *really* works or feels. The system-wide shift in the access and distribution of public knowledge has been combined with an increasing awareness that the planner has never been able to take account of the subtleties of deep *local* knowledge. As a result, the traditional intellectual tools of planning are being challenged on two fronts. Technical, system knowledge is accessible to larger numbers of people and the local, tacit knowledge of built environments is increasingly seen as beyond 'capture'.

How do we build a new professional paradigm in which planners are better able to mediate between competing demands despite their relative lack of technical and local knowledge?

Democracy and planning

We live in a world where London is better connected to New York than to Croydon. Planning is about creating and actualising visions of the future built on identity and perceived social 'need'. But relational links within and between cities, towns, places and the future have become too multiple and powerful for purely geographic notions of identity. Strong, fluid globalising identities have continually perforated the geographic boundaries of belonging. These connections are also increasingly unpredictable, with market forces and community autonomy devolving and decentralising flows of action, connection and disconnection in contemporary cities. As communities' demands for autonomy clash with national and global responsibilities, decision-making processes themselves are brought into question.

In the past, citizens accepted planning decisions because they elected and held to account the local councillors who influenced and regulated planners' work. The fragmentation of values, proliferation of communities and multiplication of democratic channels have undermined the existing frameworks of political consensus required to legitimise planning.

Where in the past councillors were in a position to take political pressure on behalf of planners, arguably, today their decisions have been overly politicised.

How do we re-articulate the legitimacy of the planner and do more to engage communities?

Beyond the plan

What possible models can we imagine for the 'future planner'?

Kill the plan – the scenario planner

To revitalise their role as change-agents driving innovation, the planner could work beyond the plan as a 'scenario planner'. Scenario planning is based on the idea that creating several alternative futures is an excellent way to manage uncertainty. Recognising the problems of 'the plan', the planner could co-create different visions of a locality's future for residents to engage with. Making important neighbourhood dynamics visible in this way, and characterising various possible responses, is a proven way to engage the public and broaden debate.

Network planning

Network planning recognises the limits of geographic democracy, where the rights of a community are not matched by responsibility to those from 'out of town'. Citizen panels chosen by lot could link the aspirations of locals and those from elsewhere by including groups of each in a citizens' jury. There have been similar, successful models of citizens' budget schemes, with communities collectively deciding on spending priorities.

Planner as judge

The planner as judge repositions the planning system away from democratic legitimacy towards 'judicial legitimacy'. In a world of multichannel democracy, planners could rediscover professional autonomy by asserting their independence to arbitrate between competing visions of the future. The Planning Inspectorate, for example, currently plays a similar role. These judges could be drawn from a range of fields that make up the emerging urbanist 'profession'. Crucially, the independent role of a judge could position the planner as less complicit in the planning system and build greater public trust.

Facilitating emergence

We could recognise the planner as an 'enabler', helping communities to 'self-build' by sharing knowledge of how the planning system works. This would shift the planning role from development control to facilitation. 'Advocacy planning' has been used widely as a means of finding a more equitable distribution of resources for groups that might otherwise be underrepresented.

The socratic planner

Our Google culture means answers are easily found but a certain monopoly on prescient *questions* remains. Planners might increasingly trade on their ability to ask great questions rather than to provide all the answers. This is the planner as a trouble-maker, charged with loosening the dogma of developers, communities and government, and helping to resolve conflicts of interests.

Elected chief planners

We vote for local councillors but the process of appointing planning officers and planners themselves is bureaucratic not democratic. Could we elect chief planners? Would this forge stronger connections between communities and place-shapers, and make planning more accountable? Where they have been introduced, for example, elected mayors have remoulded the planning process and its relationship to the electorate. Are such directly elected representatives better able to manage the tensions and complexities of today's communities?

Future planners

Demos is looking to build on these observations by inviting planners to talk about the future of their profession. These six models outlined above are based on what we have identified as important contemporary shifts affecting the legitimacy of planning. The shape of the profession can be remoulded only by innovative planners *themselves*, who seek to work with the grain of contemporary political, social and democratic change.

The plan might have disappeared, but planners don't have to go with it.

Peter Bradwell is a researcher at Demos and Inderpaul Johar is an architect at Zero-Zero Architects.

Notes

1   S Toulmin, *Cosmopolis: The hidden agenda of modernity* (Chicago: University of Chicago Press, 1992).
2   *The Planning and Compulsory Purchase Act 2004* (Norwich, TSO, 2004).
3   M Lyons, *National Prosperity, Local Choice and Civic Engagement* (London: HMSO, May 2006).

6. Towards DIY professionalism

Stress in the teaching profession

John Craig

For teachers, stress is an increasingly important issue. More teachers are taking early retirement than ever before. More teachers cite stress as a source of dissatisfaction and a reason for avoiding promotion. For many policy-makers, however, stress is a non-issue, a meaningless catch-all term for generic complaint. Research suggests that there is more to it than this.[1] The causes of growing stress in teaching relate to the subtle ways that the teaching profession has changed. If we can understand these changes, we may be in a better position to take positive steps to improve teachers' experiences of work.

Teaching is one of the most stressful jobs in the UK.[2] Over any two-year period, 40 per cent of teachers will experience 'major stress',[3] and in any given year 40 per cent of headteachers visit their doctor as a result of it.[4] Forty-four per cent of teachers say that their job is 'very' or 'extremely' stressful[5] and research shows that this is the primary reason why teachers leave the profession.[6] However, the picture is not the same in France, for example. Stress accounts for 22 per cent of UK teachers' sick leave, but just 1 per cent of French teachers'.[7] Nor, by all accounts, was stress such a problem for teachers 30 years ago. It seems, therefore, that stress is not intrinsic to work in classrooms, but is caused by certain characteristics of the education system.

However, while teachers report growing levels of stress, there is a growing body of comment that suggests that stress is good for us. It is good for us, the argument runs, to be challenged and high-quality public services depend on professionals able to meet this challenge. In this way, an implicit connection is made between growing levels of teacher stress and the rise of a 'therapy culture'. Greater reported stress is held to be itself a symptom of an increasingly self-obsessed heart-on-the-sleeve society in which rising wealth has robbed us of a sense of perspective about *real* hardship.

While there is some truth to this point of view, the ubiquitous 'stress' of conversation is very different from that which causes people to visit their doctor or leave work altogether. While it may be a source of frustration to policy-makers, the problem of stress in teaching is very real. Indeed, there is an increasingly strong body of evidence that suggests mental health will be a key problem for public policy in the coming decade.[8] To understand how this problem has grown, it helps first to see how teachers' professionalism has changed and then to understand the relationships between this professionalism and various forms of stress.

DIY professionalism

The argument we want to make is that teaching has become more stressful because teachers' personal responsibility increasingly outstrips their professional authority. Increasingly teachers have to generate their own professional status and legitimacy, and have had to become personal guardians of their own professional values. This is all the more stressful because it is at odds with the form of professionalism to which most teachers aspire.

Teachers have always aimed for a professional ethos grounded in and supported by specifically professional forms of governance. Modelling themselves on the 'elite professions' of law and medicine, teachers' professional culture encourages them to engage in a tug-of-war between their own control of education and external government or market control. Teachers continue to aspire to a collective autonomy and self-regulation to the exclusion of the market and the state.

As this collection shows, if the legal profession did achieve this kind of autonomy, it was relatively short-lived. For teachers, this period of classic professionalism was even shorter, if it existed at all.

School inspectors and universities were eroding teacher control as early as the 1950s.[9] Indeed, Robert Lowe (an education administrator in the 1860s) commented that 'teachers desiring to criticise the code were as impertinent as chickens wishing to decide the sauce in which they would be served'.[10]

However, the notion of a golden age of teacher professionalism continues to dominate teachers' professional imagination. The classroom in which the teacher is free to teach as they please, the school run by a collegial partnership of teachers and an education system free from the demands of the economy and social justice – these images remain powerful symbols in teaching. However, as a description of our changing education system, they are more inaccurate than ever. Pedagogy and curriculum depend far more on national, local and school decision-making than on teachers' own preferences. The market for school places means that schools have little time for collective decision-making and little leeway to make radical choices. And as *Every Child Matters*[11] sweeps across our education system, it is clearer than ever that the responsibilities of the education system extend far beyond learning, to socialisation, child safety, and health and community regeneration. The result of this process is a growing gap between the ideals of teacher professionalism and its reality. Given the personal importance to teachers of their work, this is in itself an important source of stress.

However, this aspiration gap is not alone sufficient to explain the levels of stress in the teaching profession. While teachers' work is increasingly being colonised by the corporate interests of public services, they continue to seek to assert their professionalism. While teachers cannot necessarily control what it is they are asked to do, they can control the norms and ethics that shape the way in which they do it. As a result, informal, cultural elements are today much more important to teachers' professionalism and formal control of teaching less so. In other words, while teachers once sought to ground their professional culture in formal structures of control, today there is a growing opposition between the structure and culture of teaching. Today it is down to teachers themselves to assert a set of values that in the past were partially embedded in the education system – to work against rather than with the grain.

We argue that this translates into professional stress in two further ways. First, teachers' professionalism is more personal than ever before. To become a professional teacher one must internalise a set of norms that cover everything from what counts as a good lesson to how best to relate to parents. It is increasingly professionalism of this kind to which colleagues look for signs of an insider and to which parents look for a guarantee of trustworthiness. However, as we shall see, this ensures that staff feel the stresses of work more deeply, have less support in coping with them and find them harder to leave behind.

Second, a teaching profession no longer able to achieve closure against external demands must constantly negotiate the terms and boundaries of its professional prerogative. Within a given local authority, for example, where teachers' responsibilities end and social workers' begin is an open question. Teachers themselves, through dialogue and through their practice, are increasingly engaged in defining their own profession. To create spaces of autonomy in which they can work, teachers increasingly depend on their own entrepreneurship. Here, stress comes from a lack of security – from constantly having to re-invent one's status and role.

This kind of professionalism demands greater personal resources and personal creativity. It is a DIY professionalism, which teachers themselves must define and build. However, DIY professionalism is not a source of stress for all teachers. For the most resilient, the challenge of developing innovative, rewarding teaching within this demanding framework has been a new lease of life. However, for those teachers with less confidence or resilience, it is an important source of additional burden and stress. We need to understand in greater detail the kinds of stress to which DIY professionalism can make teachers vulnerable.

Initiative overload and intellectual stress

The first source of growing stress is a shifting relationship between policy and practice. DIY professionalism is part of a system that has abandoned national standardisation in favour of local innovation, placing huge strategic burden on teachers themselves.

The recent white paper, for example, unleashes a range of dynamics: more competition, more collaboration, new providers and changing governance. The question of how these elements fit together and which has greatest potential is for professionals themselves to help to answer. In response, in addition to many important specific criticisms, teachers have complained that the package as a whole is 'incoherent'. Again, this seems to show teaching struggling to come to terms with DIY professionalism and the strains it inevitably involves. Forging a feasible role out of the diverse resources at their disposal is becoming teachers' own responsibility. In today's education system, coherence is not designed in by a few policy-makers, it emerges from the work of thousands of professionals.

However, this places great psychological strain on teachers themselves, especially more senior teachers. The experience of 'initiativitis' or 'initiative overload', as teachers characterise it, would be stressful at the best of times. It is even more so because it happens in the context of DIY professionalism. Where teachers take greater personal responsibility for their work, the dissonance created by reforms that pull them in many directions at once can be difficult to bear. In a sector where increasingly, 'what you do is what you are', this kind of incoherence can splinter not only the picture that professionals have of their work but also their own professional identity.

For example, the spread of market forces through our education system seems to depend for its effectiveness on the counter-balancing force of professional norms and ethics. Schools could increasingly seek to serve narrow, institutional interests, but the hope is that leaders' sense of 'moral purpose' will prevent this. The hope, in other words, is that teachers will set their face against the prevailing wind.

However, this strategy, for all the efficiency and innovation it may generate, can be intellectually exhausting for teachers.

To help teachers to build resilience in the face of this initiative overload, we need to help them to picture their place in the changing systems of children's services around them. We need to equip them with the skills of systems thinking, in which they have not been trained and which they are not encouraged to practise. In addition, we need to create experiences for teachers through which they can learn to deal with chaos and incoherence with greater confidence and resilience.

Soft governance and emotional stress

Groups like the teaching profession are increasingly accused by government of being 'producer interests' – of taking a strategic, instrumental attitude to their work in their own private interests. The suggestion of DIY professionalism is that the very opposite is happening: teachers' sense of self is more bound up with their work than ever before. While particular education policies may fail to win hearts and minds, the education system has done so hook, line and sinker. As a result, teaching is more emotionally stressful than ever before.

Teachers increasingly exert control over their work through their professional values and use these values as a key marker of colleagues' professionalism. The growth in this kind of 'soft governance' – governance through values – has been so rapid because it provides teachers with a source of personal satisfaction and is an excellent way to coordinate our increasingly complex education system. However, for teachers, it is a double-edged sword.

A key demand of professionals has always been self-regulation. Today, while collectively this is strictly limited, personally teachers are increasingly literally engaged in *self*-regulation. The most powerful regulator of teachers' practice has been their own conscience, but today this conscience is shaped by Ofsted frameworks and assessment criteria. Newly qualified teachers, for example, engage in daily personal appraisal against the public standards that they have been taught to make their own.

Crucially, this blurs the boundaries between personal and professional life. Using social conventions to regulate teachers' behaviour tugs at the heart strings in a way that does not stop at 5pm. It means that teachers are engaged in more emotional labour than ever before. The danger for some teachers is that soft governance exploits their emotional commitments, creating an exhaustion from which it is hard to find the space to recover.

In response, we need to explore the creation of new professional rituals and structures that can share some of this emotional burden. We need to shape the education system to create more supportive relationships within the teaching profession and with the teaching profession, in order to sustain the kind of emotional contribution that teachers make to our children.

Work–life balance and physical stress

Particularly for more senior teachers, the third kind of stress they face is physical. The amount of time and energy teaching takes in the average week can be physically exhausting and difficult to combine with the demands of family life. In a society in which parenting itself is increasingly a public issue with highly codified public expectations, this can be a source of real guilt and stress for teachers.

Today, parents have fewer family and community resources to draw on yet we expect them to do more than ever before – to spend more time with their children and to invest in all aspects of their development. However, this is not always compatible with professional life. For example, even today, just 60 per cent of female headteachers have children, compared with 90 per cent of male headteachers and in applying for headship they are more likely to consider family circumstances.[12]

However, as gender relations in the home gradually equalise, this is not solely an issue for women teachers. Today, all professionals are experiencing declining satisfaction with their work hours. Indeed, as their responsibilities at home grow, men in particular are growing in frustration with their working hours. The proportion of professional men satisfied with these hours fell from 36 per cent in 1992 to 16 per cent in 2002.[13] Taking headship as an example again, a growing proportion of headteachers are female. From 26 per cent in 1997 to 31 per cent in 2002, today women represent 35 per cent of headteachers.[14]

As the teaching profession ages, recruitment and retention will become vitally important public issues. In the case of headteachers, this is already happening apace. As a result, finding new solutions to the time pressures faced by families is a growing public as well as private imperative. The workforce reform agenda is very much here to stay and will need to offer teachers genuine choices that help them resolve the stress of combining professional and family life.

Conclusion

Stress in our work lives is anything but a new phenomenon and for that reason there is a natural scepticism about its rise up the political agenda. However, teachers, possibly in common with other professionals, are operating within a new set of circumstances. Teachers' professional standing has become a heavy personal responsibility, robbing them of the kind of psychological security that professionalism seems to promise to provide. As a result, in the forms of dissonance they are expected to manage, in the level of emotional labour they are expected to perform and through the challenge of combining professional and family life, teachers are vulnerable to important new sources of stress.

In response, the focus of professional demands should not be the return of teaching to a mythical era of autonomy and exclusion. The teaching profession needs new skills, rituals and career structures that will enable all staff to develop the confidence and creativity to assert their views about learning and its purpose and to make the most of the space afforded to them by their DIY professionalism.

With thanks to Alyssa Joye, Demos intern, for help with the research for this essay.

Notes

1   Research by J Craig and C Fieschi, Demos (forthcoming publication).
2   Health and Safety Executive, 'Self reported work related illness', 2003, see www.hse.gov.uk/statistics/causdis/stress.htm (accessed 22 May 2006).
3   Research by Teacherline, quoted in C Bunting, 'Stress on the emotional landscape', *Times Educational Supplement*, 10 Nov 2000, see www.tes.co.uk/section/story/?section=Archive&sub_section=Briefing&story_id =340592&Type=0 (accessed 22 May 2006).
4   Research by the National Association of Headteachers, quoted in M Jarvis, 'Teacher stress: a critical review of recent findings and suggestions for future research directions', *Stress News* 14, no 1 (Jan 2002).
5   NHS Health Scotland, *The Teachers Health and Wellbeing Study Scotland* (Edinburgh: NHS Health Scotland, 2004), see www.hebs.co.uk/researchcentre/pdf/RE045Final0203.pdf (accessed 22 May 2006).
6   A Smithers and P Robinson, *Factors Affecting Teachers' Decisions to Leave the Profession*, Research Report 430 (Nottingham: Department for Education and Skills, 2003).
7   Jarvis, 'Teacher stress'.
8   R Layard, 'Mental health: Britain's biggest social problem?', 2004, see www.strategy.gov.uk/downloads/files/mh_layard.pdf (accessed 22 May 2006).
9   G McCulloch, G Helsby and P Knight, *The Politics of Professionalism* (London: Continuum International Publishing Group, 2000).
10 Ibid.
11 HM Government, *Every Child Matters: Change for children* (HM Government, 2004), see www.everychildmatters.gov.uk/_files/F9E3F941DC8D4580539EE4C743E9371 D.pdf (accessed 22 May 2006).
12 M Coleman, *Gender and Headship in the 21st Century* (Nottingham, National College for School Leadership, 2004), see www.ncsl.org.uk/media/B13/B7/twlf-gender-and-headship.pdf (accessed 22 May 2006).
13 R Taylor, 'Britain's world of work: myths and realities', ESRC Future of Work Programme (2002), quoted in S Wise, 'Work–life balance: literature and research review', 2004, see www.napier.ac.uk/depts/eri/Downloads/LitReview.pdf (accessed 22 May 2006).
14 Coleman, *Gender and Headship in the 21st Century*.

Professional innovation

7. Journalism is itself a religion (and the faith is being tested)

Jay Rosen

If the legitimacy of a whole host of professions is being called into question, it may be that journalists are ahead of the curve. And as their situation presses them to understand their own profession better, there may be broader lessons for other professionals. In particular, I argue that the press has sought to generate two things: innocence (we do just the facts journalism) and power (we do make a difference journalism). At the best of times, any profession will find it hard to combine the benefits of activism and neutrality. In the case of the press, too few people have addressed this task at all, and even fewer in the language of democratic politics.

As it seeks to understand itself better, I suggest journalism, that secular enterprise, can best do so as a kind of religion. With that in mind, I suggest a new course: 'Understanding the priesthood of the press':

> *This course will examine the priesthood of the journalism profession in the United States, especially those at top news organisations in New York and Washington. Among the questions we'll be asking this term: How does this elite group create and maintain its authority over what counts as serious journalism? What sense of duty goes along with being one of the high priests? What are the god terms and faith objects in journalism, and how are they derived?*

You get the idea. There is a high church in journalism, with high ceremonies, like the awarding of a Pulitzer Prize.

Once at the Columbia J-School I told the graduates they had passed through not only a great professional training ground in journalism, but a 'great school of theology'. 'It's like a divinity degree,' I said. Only rarely does a public speaker know that the audience as a whole 'got' something. This was one of those times. At the words 'school of theology', I saw a very large number of alumni smile or nod. They could recall it in their experience. Smart people entering the profession learn the religion of journalism. Amid their practical lessons they acquire their faith in a free press.

They also absorbed a sense of what's sacred, what's profane in journalism, as with the wall between the news and business sides of the operation. The wall is commonly called the 'separation of church and state' by newsroom pros, who speak metaphorically yet with great passion and precision about this sacred divide. And who is the church in that comparison? It isn't the counting room, it's the newsroom. The church is supposed to be journalism. The money side is of course profane.

Ninety per cent of the commentary on this subject takes in another kind of question entirely: What results from the 'relative godlessness of mainstream journalists'? Here and there in the discussion of religion 'in' the news, there arises a trickier matter, which is the religion of the newsroom, and of the priesthood in the press. A particularly telling example began with this passage from a 1999 *New York Times* magazine article about anti-abortion extremism: 'It is a shared if unspoken premise of the world that most of us inhabit that absolutes do not exist and that people who claim to have found them are crazy,' wrote David Samuels.[1]

In other words, it's against newsroom religion to be an absolutist and in this sense, the Isaiah Berlin sense, the press is a liberal institution put in the uncomfortable position of being 'closed' to other traditions and their truth claims – specifically, the orthodox faiths.

The apparent orthodoxy of forbidding all orthodoxies has been a philosophical puzzle in liberalism since John Locke. Journalists cannot be expected to solve it. However, they might in some future professional climate (which may be around the corner) come to examine the prevailing orthodoxy about journalism – how to do it, name it, explain it, uphold it and protect it – for that orthodoxy does exist. And it does not always have adequate answers. For this examination to happen, journalists will need to understand their profession more deeply and to talk and think together about the basis of the work they do.

Press religion: the First Amendment and Watergate

As a religion, American journalism, as we would expect, has a founding myth; and it has long used this myth to generate leverage and legitimacy.

Within the press religion, there is one matter on which it is permitted to be an absolutist in the newsroom. You can even be admired for it. And that is First Amendment absolutism, with its obvious appeal to journalists. Hands off the media in the name of the public's right to know! This is the biblical lesson most journalism students absorb. The lesson is totally right in its sphere, but it is only one kind of wisdom.

Journalists also need to grasp how the press does – or does not – foster the kind of quality debate required if people are to make democracy work. They should see how it's possible for the press, when a concentrated industry overtakes it, to be a barrier to entry, even as it overflows with good information. Free and unfettered, the press can shut people out, ignore their views, or unfairly constrict debate. It can decide that two candidates matter tonight, not five. It can refuse free air time to a leader with a message.

These are serious First Amendment issues, but they make a weak impression in the grand story of press freedom drawn from Watergate. In the newsroom faith that I have been describing, Watergate is not just a big, big story with a knock-out ending, it is the great redemptive story believers learn to tell about the press and what it can do for the American people. It is a story of national salvation: truth their only weapon, journalists save the day. Whether the story can continue to claim enough believers – and connect the humble to the heroic in journalism – is to my mind a big question. Whether it should continue is an even better question.

When the press took over the legend of Watergate, the main characters were no longer the bad guys like Richard Nixon, who broke the law and abused state power. The narrative got turned around. Watergate became a story about heroism at the *Washington Post*. The protagonists were Woodward and Bernstein, with Nixon a character in their play.

From press scholar Michael Schudson:

> *Watergate, by forcing a president to resign, was an exploding supernova in the sky of journalism, blotting out the record of investigative work during Vietnam. It was not only more salient,* it was more consensual. *Seymour Hersh's work in uncovering the My Lai massacre was too bloody and devastating and divisive a report to hold up as the epitome of American enterprise journalism. Watergate, at least retrospectively, could be accepted as a triumph not only of American journalism but of the American system of a free press.*[2] *(Emphasis mine. That was 1992; see Schudson's comments on the Felt revelation.*[3]*)*

He's right: the myth of Watergate sustains an entire press system, including its thought system: 'It was more consensual,' Schudson says of the scandal. What Nixon and his henchmen did wrong is wrong by consensus – or even acclamation. It's like mom and apple pie in reverse. Therefore what the *Washington Post* did during Watergate is right by consensus, or even acclamation. And who doesn't want to be right like that? Who wouldn't want to sustain it?

The myth of Watergate presents the press as a powerful force but also an innocent one because its only weapon is uncovering truth – to expose corruption, give voice to the downtrodden. One of the reasons Watergate doesn't go away is this spectacular production of innocence, which is supposed to serve as a force field against charges of agenda-serving.

It is also a case the press 'won', as was the Pentagon Papers, a related case. By winning key cases in the 1960s and 1970s, the press was expanding its power to stand up to government. And that is where the religion directs our attention: to struggles with the state. These, according to the faith, are really victories for the public and its right to know.

A religion starting to fail

There are a range of ways in which this professional religion fails journalism and the public, and these failures are becoming more serious. Politically, it is less effective and less legitimate than it has ever been.

As Matt Welch points out:

> *Much of George Bush's governing philosophy has been shaped by men (especially Dick Cheney and Donald Rumsfeld) whose worldviews are anchored at least in part to the various scandals (and reactions to same) of the mid-1970s. Like Wolfowitzian democracy-promotion, Sept. 11 gave fresh oxygen to their long-held conviction that post-Watergate reforms 'tied the hands' of the CIA and FBI, put the Executive Branch on the defensive, and handcuffed America's ability to get her hands a little dirty in the name of making the world a safer place for democracy.*[4]

This Welch calls Watergate blowback,[5] to which I would add the same sprucing up of the executive's powers, and its move towards de-certifying the press as interlocutor.

In this context, an emphasis on the consensual neutrality of the press is becoming less and less effective. For many years I taught in my criticism classes that pointing out bias in the news media was an important, interesting and even subversive activity. At the very least an intellectual challenge. Now it is virtually meaningless. Media bias is a proxy in countless political fights and the culture war. It's effectiveness as a corrective is virtually zero.

However, journalists still rely on the religion of the press to secure their role as tribunes of the people. Indeed, part of the problem with press religion is that people go on believing it regardless of its effectiveness. Investigative reporting, exposing public corruption and carrying the mantle of the downtrodden are political acts in themselves, in which the cleansing light of publicity is a weapon of reform, but in the newsroom creed these are presented more simply: a way of being idealistic, a non-political truth-teller pursuing the public good.

For James W Carey, the First Amendment says not simply 'hands off the press' but 'that people are free to gather together without the intrusion of the state or its representatives. Once gathered, they are free to speak to one another openly and freely. They are further free to write down what they have to say and to share it beyond the immediate place of utterance.'[6]

The public need help if they are going to participate and gain active voice in their own affairs. Here the press often decides who gets heard, and when. In debates, it asks the questions that get asked of the candidates. What restrictions does it enforce? How difficult is it for dissenting views to be heard? If the press in some ways 'runs' public discussion, what's to prevent a free press from running it into the ground? The religion doesn't really have answers to these questions. 'Hands off the press!' won't cut it.

'For the people to write down what they say and share it.' From this right that belongs to all citizens, Carey derives both the original meaning of press freedom, and the most urgent purpose of journalism – to amplify, clarify and extend what the rest of us produce as a 'society of conversationalists'. Public conversation is not the pundits or professionals we see on talk shows. It is 'ours to conduct', as Carey puts it. The press should help us out. Here emerges his different faith. For when 'the press sees its role as limited to informing whomever happens to turn up at the end of the communication channel, it explicitly abandons its role as an agency for carrying on the conversation of the culture'.

The conversation of the culture is today carrying on with or without the traditional press. As the power to publish shifts around, the growth of blogs is adding to journalism and commentary a gift economy, so different from the scarcity template that dominated during the age of big media. The press system is more open to amateurs. Consumers are becoming producers, readers can be writers.[7]

As a result, consensus is breaking apart on definitions of 'the good' in journalism. I used to teach it implicitly: journalism is a profession. Now I think it's a practice, in which pros and amateurs both participate. There were good things about the professional model, and we should retain them. But it's the strength of the social practice that counts, not the health of any so-called profession. That is what J-schools should teach and stand for, I believe. I don't care if they're called professional schools. They should equip the American *people* to practise journalism by teaching the students who show up, and others out there who may want help.

The god term of journalism is the public

In Carey's world the religion of the press is properly rooted in the public: 'The god term of journalism – the be-all and end-all, the term without which the enterprise fails to make sense – is the public. Insofar as journalism is grounded, it is grounded in the public.' If they, the journalists, are supposed to believe in 'us', the public, then do we, the public, have to believe in the press? That seems to me a puzzle involving in the last analysis faith.

And in fact, they wanted the innocence (we do just the facts journalism) and the power (we do make a difference journalism) but this could never be. We in the J-schools failed to catch that. The people with press cards who felt themselves on a mission never got around to justifying their mission in the language of democratic politics. They talked about it as a neutral public service instead, but speaking truth to power isn't neutral, and making a difference isn't just a service to others. We in the J-schools didn't do well with that, either.

We're headed, I think, for schism, tumult and divide as the religion of the American press meets the upheavals in global politics and public media that are well under way. (Not to mention the roaring force of the market.) Changing around us are the terms on which authority can be established by journalists.

As these changes accelerate, continued faith in the press is far from a sure thing. However, if journalists can expand the circle to include 'the people formerly known as the audience' (that's what I call them) then their religion may eventually adjust to take account of the news actors. We may yet find ways for the freedoms of press and public to grow together.

Jay Rosen is an associate professor at the Department of Journalism, New York University.

Notes

1 D Samuels, 'The making of a fugitive', *New York Times*, 21 Mar 1999.
2 M Schudson, *Watergate and American Memory* (New York: Basic Books, 1992).
3 See http://journalism.nyu.edu/pubzone/weblogs/pressthink/2005/06 /05/wtrg_js.html#comment18255 (accessed 21 May 2006).
4 See www.reason.com/hitandrun/2005/06/why_watergate_m.shtml#009746 (accessed 21 May 2006).
5 See www.reason.com/0408/co.mw.watergate.shtml (accessed 21 May 2006).
6 See http://archives.cjr.org/year/98/2/pubnote.asp (accessed 21 May 2006).
7 See http://journalism.nyu.edu/pubzone/weblogs/pressthink/2003/10/16/ radical_ten.html (accessed 21 May 2006).

8. Tomorrow's workers, yesterday's trades

Tom Wilson

Yesterday's trades are arguably today's professions. As the union movement develops, many of its constituents are becoming as concerned with learning and capacity-building as they are with pay and problem-solving. As professions grow and open up and professionalism itself becomes as much a state of mind as a status, unions are playing increasingly significant roles in processes of professionalisation. As they do so, they are beginning to offer new models of workplace organisation. They are also serving to emphasise the nineteenth-century union slogan 'Educate, Agitate, Organise'.

Long-standing professional demands

The idea of professionalism, and professional identity, is deeply important to millions of working people. Indeed, in conversation about professionalism, the term is now applied as equally to train drivers or secretaries as to airline pilots or managers. However, in practice, professional pride and demands are neither recent nor exclusively white collar.

Professional pride in a given craft or vocation has been a constant feature of the trade union movement. Within the UK, the tradition of organisation around occupational identity (rather than, for example, industrial sector) and the aspiration for better occupational recognition has always been particularly strong. This reflects a cardinal principle of organising, which is that like recruits like.

Teachers want to join teachers' unions, just as carpet weavers wanted to joint the carpet weavers' union. The UK labour movement is based on *trades* unions.

The history of trade unionism in the UK is in part the story of working people, intensely proud of their skill or trade, seeking access to the ranks of professionals. They have organised to seek recognition and control of standards, entry and training. In this sense, trade unionism has been at least as much about joining professions as opposing them. This aspiration to professional status was (and still is) often ridiculed by those already securely in the professions (such as writers and broadcasters) as an attempt by the lower orders to gain social status. It can equally be seen as a perfectly sensible attempt to gain more secure employment and better pay and conditions, as well as more interesting jobs involving more skill, learning and autonomy.

As an example of these professional aspirations, the union movement has always been somewhat ambiguous about even the word 'union'. Of the 26 unions affiliated to the Trades Union Congress (TUC) in 1936 within the Mining and Quarrying group, 13 were actually associations. It was true of the great majority of the then 200 affiliated unions, the vast majority of which organised very specific skilled and semi-skilled trades. Of course many of these organisations were very small but in total they organised over half of all members; while there were already giant unions like the Transport and General Workers' Union and the National Union of General and Municipal Workers, even these had strong occupationally specific trade groups within their structure. The pride in occupational skill was and is very strong, and it was something that all kinds of unions had to accommodate.

Fast-growing unions are professional unions

Today, these professional aspirations are more significant than ever and unions that emphasise them are growing while others decline. In part, they are growing with the professions they represent. However, individuals are also actively choosing those unions that focus on professional issues. In doing so, they are helping to change unionism.

In part, the growth of professional unions is inevitable. Managers and administrators grew from 14 per cent of the workforce in 1991 to 16 per cent in 1999, while professionals grew from 9 per cent to 11 per cent.[1] It is commonly accepted that tomorrow's economy will require more highly skilled and more flexible workers, able to re-skill frequently. Furthermore, being a member of a union is an increasingly professional phenomenon. The 2005 *Labour Force Survey* revealed that 49 per cent of professional and managerial staff are unionised, against only 21 per cent for 'elementary occupations'.[2] (This is not something to celebrate of course; the union movement should and does seek to organise all working people, professional or not, but the fact is that the typical union member is now a graduate level woman.)

However, there is also a small but clear substitution effect – in some cases unions that focus on professional issues are growing at the expense of others. It is striking how quickly some of the newer and smaller professionals' unions are growing. It suggests that while overall union membership continues to decline, reports of the demise of UK trade unionism are somewhat premature. Professionals are finding unions that they feel look after their interests extremely well. Tomorrow's workers are increasingly thriving in the equivalent of yesterday's trades.

Professional unions

The fastest-growing unions place great emphasis on members' occupational identity, professional claims and professional development. As a result, although as unions they are relatively small and specialist, they tend to have excellent membership coverage in their chosen area.

Workers are smart. White collar and professional workers see very clearly, perhaps sometimes more clearly than their unions, that their future careers depend on skills and lifelong learning. This is creating new demands to which unions are under pressure to respond.

Helping them to do so, new government funding and the new legal right for union learning representatives (ULRs) have helped some unions to create a much more expansive role in professional development.

Today, as a result, all unions are pressing ever more strongly for better investment in professional learning and better rights to staff training. They know, for example, that French and American employers spend twice as much per employee as those in the UK on training. There are a growing number of resolutions to the TUC Congress and, though to a lesser extent, training is more likely than in previous years to feature in negotiations with employers. This is partly a result of the much greater profile given to union learning by the TUC and government, but mainly due to clear evidence that members (and potential members) want help to access learning opportunities.

However, the way in which unions organise learning varies. In some unions, the learning needs of members are greater and more specialised and union members and their places of work are strongly engaged with professional learning. These are the conditions in which small, specialised unions are growing fastest today. Professionals' unions of this kind tend to build steadily on what they already have, giving higher priority to learning in their publications, negotiating agreements with employers – for example on paid time off – and developing further their own training or continuing professional development (CPD) offer.

These unions seem able to build on and develop a sense of occupational efficacy and identity that is particularly strong. In 2005, 12 white collar and professional unions were surveyed about the issues members most cared about and which services were most valued.[3] Tying in equal place for the most important were pay and CPD – illustrating not just the importance of CPD to them but that this group of unions were perceived by their members as being able to do something about the issue they clearly rated as of equal importance to pay. Again, the 'service' rated as highly important in all 12 unions was keeping up with professional issues. Closely allied to it was that many of the unions reported that a strong sense of professional identity (which is, of course, not a 'service') was one of the most important benefits of belonging to the union.

Where in the past unions may have struggled to persuade employees that they were an important source of learning and advancement, newer, more specialised professional unions seem to be succeeding in creating a virtuous circle of success and confidence. Existing members like professional learning; it attracts new members; it attracts a newer, younger and more diverse kind of activist; employers like it; this government funds it and it helps unions grow. It is this virtuous circle that is driving their growth.

Familiar cycle or new departure?

How significant is this growth of small, specialist professional unions? In part, this is how unions have always developed. However, changes in union practice and operating environment of which this shift is a part may represent a broader professionalisation of working life in the UK.

Looking at the history of some unions, there is some evidence of a 'natural' migration; many professionals and specialists unions begin as staff associations with limited aspirations, gradually become more independent and assertive, often then affiliate to the TUC, then settle down into being medium-sized strong unions or merge to form a semi-autonomous section of a larger union. The whole journey seems to take between 20 and 40 years.

Equally, it would be grossly simplistic to conclude from this: 'general bad, specialist good'. For example, non-specialist unions such as the Public and Commercial Services Union or the National Union of Rail, Maritime and Transport Workers also grew, showing that professionals' unions were not the only model for growth. Union size still clearly matters. Larger unions have far greater resources and strength at members' disposal. For some workers, particularly in less professional or skilled occupations, occupational identity may matter less. For them, power in the labour market derives from being part of a large union rather than their specialist status. The issue in practice is often one of balancing specialist identity within an overall cohesive framework – for example by having specialist committees or pages within the union journal dedicated to particular groups.

However, the dynamics of size versus specialisation and union growth and decline are constantly changing, reflecting the demands of members. The new significance of professional learning in unions may mark a shift in their development and public position, but it is too early to be certain. The question is whether it is driving a new alignment between unions' aspirations and organisational forms and those of their members. Certainly, the learning in the most professional unions is naturally specialist, self-directed and networked, both socially and online – it may be driving just the kinds of changes within unions that are vital in adapting to the twenty-first century.

Two examples help to flesh out this possibility. First, the Association of Teachers and Lecturers has recently invested heavily in organising, appointing a lead organising officer with seven staff. Historically, the union had relied on a relatively less well-developed branch and activist structure; traditionally, it had relied more than other teaching unions on 'servicing' from caseworker officers or head office. But having surveyed members it found they wanted more sense of belonging and involvement (occupational identity and organising) and more union engagement in learning – CPD opportunities and in-service training. These were what members valued but the major obstacle was time – work hours and childcare. So those issues are now being very actively taken up with employers. At the same time the union journal has been revamped and more attention is being given to professional issues such as school organisation, discipline and the curriculum. Interestingly, this shift towards increased emphasis on professional issues has gone hand in hand with a more robust and assertive attitude towards employers and government, for example over proposed legislation on schools. Professionalism does not mean political passivity.

Second, the 31,000 strong Musicians' Union has completely changed its internal organisation. It scrapped geographically based branches in favour of musical specialism-based branches. Thus there is a national jazz branch, classical branch, session guitar branch and so forth. Again, this was the result of intensive membership debate which found that members did not really value the chance to meet other members unless they were engaged in the same branch of the business. Moreover very few members attended branch meetings since communication, for example by phone or email, was quite adequate. Again, the union journal has been radically revamped to give a greater profile to 'professional' issues, interviews with celebrity members and so forth – though pay and contract issues are still very important. CPD has always been central to a musician's life and the new journal and internal organisation put more emphasis on this.

Conclusion

Time will tell, but there is a possibility that professionalisation is working hand in hand with important background changes in trade unionism.

Two shifts in unions' operating environments are particularly important to highlight. First, as knowledge becomes more important across our economy, learning is increasingly specialist, self-directed and networked. Second, as organisational environments become more complex and devolved, complicating surveillance, some employers are finding that models of control are having to be replaced by models of negotiation. Set alongside declining social barriers to the professions and new opportunities to network their staff, these represent important opportunities for union development.

While, as we have seen, today's new professional unions may grow more like their larger counterparts, there is another possibility. The focus on professionalism drives unions to satisfy individual ambition and public legitimacy, alongside members' collective interests.[4]

Amid these changing circumstances, unions may find new ways to align the interests of employers, public and members, expanding their own significance.

Analysts are split about tomorrow's labour force. For some, it will resemble an hour glass – split between large numbers of highly skilled and rewarded workers and equally large numbers of workers excluded from these salaries and opportunities. For others, the labour force will look more like a plant pot, with a broader range of salaries and positions and greater mobility between them. Successful unions are, and will increasingly be, those which are able to help members get that lifelong learning, either by providing it directly or by encouraging employers and governments to do so. They will be the ones that help to build a plant pot-shaped workforce and help their members to ascend it. Unions are learning from this the importance of putting a strong emphasis on identity, trade and profession, and demonstrating a concern to help members keep up with learning and CPD.

In the process, they may change the image and public position of unions. From being seen as a source of cost to firms and economies in the short term, this may help with the recognition of their role in driving investment for the long term. Equally, as individuals seek to cope with a rapidly changing economy and world of work, unions may come to be seen as much in terms of preparation for (and ambitions for) tomorrow as defence of a status quo.

To face the future, we must go back to our roots, to the need to Educate, as well as Agitate and Organise; and to the fact that we organise as *trades* unions. In a world where we can all be professionals, this may be more significant than ever.

Tom Wilson is Head of the Organisation and Services Department at the TUC.

Notes

1   *Quarterly Labour Force Survey*, SOEC dataset, December 1999 – February 2000, see www.data-archive.ac.uk/findingData/snDescription.asp?sn=4439 (accessed 26 May 2006).

2   Office for National Statistics, *Trade Union Membership 2005* (London: Department of Trade and Industry, 2006), available at www.dti.gov.uk/files/file25737.pdf (accessed 21 May 2006).

3   Association of College Management Survey, quoted in 'Time for a "work–learn" balance, says TUC survey', see www.tuc.org.uk/skills/tuc-9976-f0.cfm (accessed 26 May 2006).
4   T Loveless (ed), *Conflicting Missions? Teacher unions and educational reform* (Washington, DC: Brookings Institution Press, 2000).

9. Governance and the analytic institution

Helen Morgan

Introduction

This is a long moment of uncertainty in the profession of psychoanalysis and psychotherapy. The mills that move us towards state registration are grinding exceedingly slowly and churning up the hard grist of how we define ourselves, what we do, what we don't do, which lines are to be drawn and where, who will be on which side and what we will all end up being called. Current struggles include concerns of status, economics, authority and identity, but also a heartfelt urge to protect a certain way of thinking and working that is much under attack at the moment.

The complex politics of what I shall be referring to as the profession of psychoanalytic psychotherapy may seem tiny against the backdrop of those struggling in the public sector and some may question whether this private, privileged and parochial world has any relevance for those working 'out there' at the coal face.

I suggest it has. Put most simply, at the centre of the psychoanalytic endeavour is a relationship between two people, the analytic couple. It is the very privilege of being able to explore that relationship in a relatively uncluttered, protected, boundaried place and time that allows it to be of use beyond the therapeutic work with an individual as it offers insight into what sort of structure a therapeutic relationship is best contained within. Whatever the helping profession we are considering, we need a system that fosters authentic, trustworthy and autonomous professionals able to bear anxiety, hopelessness, powerlessness, to not-know and yet to keep on thinking. In many ways, what is happening to psychoanalytic psychotherapy is a particularly heightened or extreme version of what is happening to other professions. The dilemmas and choices are not radically different, only starker.

Alone in the presence of . . .

Analysis takes place within a container. The free associating of the analysand, the reverie of the analyst and the play between them can happen only in a space where confidentiality and privacy are secure and trusted. The analytic couple *must* be alone in order for analysis to take place. However, in this aloneness each becomes vulnerable to the other and there is the real risk that privacy slips into dangerous secrecy. Boundaries may crumble and the unconscious vengeful or erotic forces may overwhelm leading to the loss of the analyst's agapaic, ethical and analytical attitude resulting in retaliation and acting out. It is, therefore, also imperative that this analytic couple are *not* alone.

Winnicott proposes that the capacity to be alone is a crucial aspect of healthy development and that this happens through the infant being able to be alone *in the presence of* the mother. As he states:

> Here is implied a rather special type of relationship, that between the infant or small child who is alone, and the mother or mother-substitute who is in fact reliably present even if represented for the moment by a cot or a pram or the general atmosphere of the immediate environment.[1]

Winnicott is, of course, speaking of the individual infant alone with its mother. When he writes, albeit sparingly, about the paternal role he also hints at a notion of this 'nursing couple' itself being alone in the presence of a third. This 'third' is the 'other' in whose presence the mother/infant couple are alone. This 'other' has the dual role of protecting the couple from external impingements, but also to intervene at times of stress between them. Applying this to the analytic couple, the image I'm presenting is that of their being alone together *in the presence of* an 'other', and that this 'other' is the analytic institution.

If we now return to Winnicott but substitute the analytic couple for the infant:

> *It is only when alone (that is to say in the presence of someone) that the infant can discover his own personal life. The pathological alternative is a false life built on reactions to external stimuli. When alone in the sense that I am using the term, and only when alone, the infant is able to do the equivalent of what in an adult would be called relaxing.*[2]

In a sense, of course, this notion of 'alone in the presence of . . .' is merely a reformulation of the concept of the analyst's internalised good objects gained hopefully through their own analysis, supervision and general training. But changing the image slightly shifts attention from the particular practitioner to that of the profession as a whole. For then the question becomes how the profession should best be organised so that it can be the facilitative, concerned and benign 'other' in whose presence the analytic couple can be alone. The intention is an 'aloneness' that allows them to 'rediscover the personal impulse' rather than the 'pathological alternative' of 'a false life built on reactions to external stimuli'.

The traditional profession

As with all professions, that of psychoanalysis has its own internal system of professional authority and responsibility held by people who are assumed to know their craft. They are the 'elders' who hold authority in the realms of gate-keeping, assessment, teaching, ethics and so on because of their experience and expertise.

However, unlike other professions, psychoanalysis has as yet no established system of external reference; there are few links to academia and the research base is developing but still weak. Even within a fairly narrow definition of psychoanalysis, there are a number of theoretical approaches, a variety of 'truths', each avowed by different groupings with historical and current conflicts between them. While other professionals operate in a more open forum so their work is publicly available to be judged, the very privacy of this one makes assessment a more intricate affair. The analytic profession has existed in relative isolation, arranged in a hierarchy as a hermetically sealed system unaccountable to any external body. The profession has, I suggest, itself been left too much alone for too long.

It has, of course, its critics both from within and from without. In his book entitled *Unfree Associations*, Kirsner, who conducted a major piece of research into analytic institutions in America, refers to the 'clubbishness, internal focus, anointment and fratricidal behaviour in psychoanalytic cultures'.[3]

Kirsner is especially critical of the system of training analysts, which elevates certain elders within the hierarchy and gives them control of assessment, training, the 'rules' of the institution and the process he refers to as 'anointment' of the favoured few. The argument is that the system of training analysts establishes and reinforces an ideal, a sort of 'super-analyst' who is the only one trusted to analyse candidates and have overall control within the institution. Only some will make it to this idealised state yet the skills, qualities and competencies necessary for selection to these and other ranks are rarely made explicit.

In his paper 'The analytic super-ego', Colman refers to the similarity between analytic training and initiation rites and the tendency this creates for candidates to 'remodel' themselves in the image of their community's ideal. The candidate's ego-ideal is thus transformed into an analytic ego-ideal to be monitored by an analytic super-ego identified with the analytic community at large.[4]

It is inevitable that there is a degree of idealisation of those who, after all, we spend a great deal of time and money training to become like. However, the greater the gap between the ideal and the reality, the greater the threat of shame and the harsher the super-ego response. Denigration of the so-called elders while appearing to refute their power is merely the other side of the same emotional coin. Both idealisation and denigration are exacerbated by distance and by the desired qualities and abilities being kept undefined and opaque. If the qualities of these elders, the training analysts, the supervisors, the teachers, are assumed but not defined, and the criteria for assessing the various stages of career development not explicit, then qualification and later progress becomes a haphazard business of unknown factors and/or the benign regard of those with power.

Eldership and governance

A shift towards greater transparency *is* happening but, I suggest, *only* because of the external demands of governance on the analytic institutions. Thus far I see these demands as having a positive, opening effect on the profession. Indeed, like a series of 'Russian dolls' it might be seen to be an external 'other', in whose presence it can be alone.

Instead of thinking of actual 'elders' with all the implications of an idealised aristocracy or elite, I want to put forward the idea of 'eldership' as a functional attribute or quality essential to any profession. This includes the particulars of the craft, the theoretical framework, its moral code, its wisdom. While represented by certain individuals at any one time, its ownership and development need to be accepted as the responsibility of all members – including candidates in training. In the wider profession, in any analytic institution, and also in any individual practitioner, both functions of eldership and of governance need to operate in relationship to each other. It's that relationship I wish to explore briefly here. To do so I need to change language for a moment.

The British Association of Psychotherapists, like similar organisations, is managed by a council elected from and by the membership. The tasks of the organisation relating to its objectives are delegated to the various committees and they carry out the day-to-day business in dialogue with the council through the various representatives. In the set of papers each council member is given on

joining, governance is defined as 'the systems and processes concerned with ensuring the overall direction, effectiveness, supervision
and accountability of an organisation'.

Currently corporate governance requirements from external bodies
apply on account of the fact that we are a charity and a company
limited by guarantee, making council members both trustees and
directors with specific legal responsibilities for compliance with:

○ charity law and the requirements of the Charity
  Commission
○ company law and the requirements of Company House
○ employment law
○ health and safety legislation
○ data protection legislation
○ legislation against discrimination on grounds of race,
  disability, gender and other factors.

As with any profession, the tasks of the analytic institution need to be
undertaken in a way that ensures that the aspects of governance and
those of eldership are in a respectful relationship with each other.
However, I see this as an asymmetrical relationship with the function
of governance acting as the container for that of eldership. Good
governance acts as the 'other', which protects eldership from external
impingement but may also need to intervene at times and require it
to make itself known and understandable. Again the metaphor of
'alone' in the presence of the other seems apposite here. Indeed good
governance – as opposed to government – refers in part to that
balancing act between intruding and enabling.

Mostly, of course, the work of the organisation goes on without
serious conflict between the two functions. The more profound
disputes tend to be those which concern difference relating to matters
of eldership. Here there is usually a subtext regarding professional
recognition, authority, power and status. Then each side, in pursuit of
what they believe to be right, may challenge those aspects of
governance which are seen not to suit, and ultimately, therefore,

council's *function*. However, it is the requirement to hold to agreed constitutional policies and procedures and to be accountable to democracy within the membership as well as external demands that can and should act as the container for the internal debate.

Governance and state regulation

So far I have been referring to a benign definition of governance as a helpful, opening effect on the analytic institution. However, the starting point of the metaphor is the aloneness of the infant. The infant needs the mother's presence so he or she can forget it and get on with the developmental work of relaxing. His play or his reverie should not be intruded on by an over-anxious mother who is constantly poking him to check he is OK. Similarly, the analytic couple must be alone to get on with their own particular form of relaxing. They must be protected from the intrusion of a judgemental, shame-inducing analytic ego-idea, but also from the invasion by an over-anxious system of governance which has little capacity to trust this aloneness and wants to manage and control it quite directly by intruding into it. Governance now becomes not the presence the practitioner and client can be alone within, but the paranoid intruder that is driven by anxiety and fails to trust.

The government's current plan is that the professions of psychoanalysis, psychotherapy and counselling will eventually be registered within the Health Professions Council. Currently this sets standards for 12 health professions including radiographers, clinical scientists, arts therapists, dieticians and others.

It is hard to be clear at this stage what the implications for this profession are going to be. Glancing across at those sister professions that are already state regulated and seeing the tidal wave of governance requirements, which seem to be almost drowning the practitioner in anxiety-driven, risk-averse, overly rational demands, I admit to a worry that this over-controlling ethos will find it hard to leave the analytic couple alone.

Of what we know already there is much concern about the question of how complaints against practitioners on ethical grounds are likely to be heard. As things stand currently this is by a committee made up of practitioners from a rotation within the 12 registered professions plus a number of lay members. This means that a complaint against a psychoanalytic psychotherapist may be heard by a panel that includes only one or possibly two from the profession. It is unlikely, therefore, that there will be much understanding of unconscious processes or the transference. Cases are also heard in open court which means anyone can attend – including the press. As soon as a complaint is made it is published on the internet as a case pending, including the names of both the therapist and the patient.

This is too much light on the subject. Such procedures fail to recognise the particular nature of psychoanalytic work and could actually weaken the governance of the profession since it may mean that many patients will fear making a complaint as, if they do, the work of the analysis, and therefore of themselves, will no longer be private. Some may make a complaint as an attack on their analyst as they will be publicly named even before the case is heard. Where there are grounds for complaint, the process of doing so can be a deeply painful process for a patient and needs to be managed in a safe, confidential and careful place by people who have an understanding of unconscious processes. This includes an understanding that an analyst who repeatedly extends the session, gives gifts, goes to the patient's home and so on is not being generous and helpful, as it might appear to an external observer, but is actually transgressing boundaries and breaking an important trust between them.

As we often discover in analysis itself, what one sets out to do, our conscious intention, has this odd way of having the exact opposite effect. As Bauman says:

> *You want to legislate the quality of life and you get this funny problem that the receptive, spontaneous aspects of the quality of life would be lost if you legislated it.*[5]

Now it is the function of eldership that must come to the fore to challenge governance and insist on the need for opacity. It is what understands the space that the other wishes to intrude into, trusts it and knows that damage will be done by careless interference.

End thought

Whether we like it or not state regulation is inevitable. But it's a difficult process, raising as it does all sorts of conflicts within the profession, but also within oneself. One minute I'm the rebel shaking my fist at this self-appointed, frequency-obsessed, rigid elite, and the next I'm one of the elders tut-tutting at the poor 'standards' of others.

What I want to do is to retreat back into the privacy and aloneness of my consulting room. But there is no retreat, there is always the 'other' that has to be engaged with. If we don't speak out for good eldership and good governance, then the psychoanalytic way of thinking may be reduced to a tiny corner of our world. And that, I do believe, would be detrimental to us all.

Helen Morgan is Chair of the British Association of Psychotherapists.

Notes

1   DW Winnicott, *The Maturational Processes and the Facilitating Environment* (London: Karnac, 1995).
2   Ibid.
3   D Kirsner, *Unfree Associations: Inside psychoanalytic institutes* (London: Process Press, 1999).
4   W Colman, 'The analytic super-ego', paper given at a British Association of Psychotherapists scientific meeting, 2006, see www.jungiananalysts.org.uk/event.htm (accessed 26 May 2006).
5   Z Bauman, *Postmodern Ethics* (Oxford: Blackwell, 1993).

10. Promoting the global accountancy professional

Allan Blewitt

ACCA (the Association of Chartered Certified Accountants) believes that professionalism is the dedication to an occupation requiring a high level of skill, and commitment to a set of principles at the heart of which lies the public interest. The threshold level of skill is benchmarked using some form of evaluation, for example examinations. In many cases, the greater the skill required to practise in that profession, the more rigorous the threshold level of skill required. Ongoing professionals are expected to keep both knowledge and skills updated. The more established professions formed professional bodies, such as ACCA, to support their fellow members, set and maintain standards, and also to ensure that public interest was kept at the fore.

ACCA is the largest and fastest-growing international accountancy body with 260,000 students and 110,000 members in 170 countries. We aim to offer first choice qualifications to people of application, ability and ambition around the world who seek a rewarding career in accountancy, finance and management. With a predominantly young and dynamic membership, we aim to create value for the profession and the business community through standards and services that are innovative, relevant and of the highest possible quality.

Does it really matter?

Is this concept and value of the professional relevant in the current knowledge society? Today's consumer and business person has generally been educated to a higher level than was the case in the nineteenth century when the well-known professions of accountancy, law and medicine were established. At the beginning of the nineteenth century, the professions consisted of the church, law, medicine and the military. The industrial revolution changed that. It ushered in new occupations, which included actuaries, architects, dentists, engineers, pharmacists, veterinarians – and, naturally, accountants. These groups wanted to be recognised as professional and formed themselves into specialist bodies to help them achieve this aim.

Thanks to the likes of Microsoft and Google, the public now has near instant access to the highly sophisticated information and knowledge that was once available only to qualified professionals. Access to specialised relevant information was once the preserve of the professionals. Indeed, access to information and technology has meant that in some instances there are tasks, such as tax returns, conveyancing and probate, which the public can perform, up to a certain level, without the intervention of a professional. The outstanding question here is the exercise of professional judgement in more complex matters.

The reputation of professions – and in particular, the accountancy profession – has not benefited from the major scandals over the last decade or so. For example, the scandals that involved Enron, WorldCom and Parmalat have all challenged the accountancy profession. In this climate, the mysticism that once surrounded professionals and the deference with which they were treated has been largely replaced by scepticism. The term professionalism is further challenged given public perceptions of the group of people who comprise 'the professions' – a recent survey showed that 40 per cent of 18–29-year-olds questioned included movie acting as a profession.[1] Given this climate – what does the future hold?

The twenty-first-century professional

Globalisation, hyper-competition, unrelenting technological advancements and increased scrutiny and regulation results in a complex environment in which to do business. It is easy for entrepreneurs and managers alike to find that they are spending more time trying to de-clutter their business environment and manage risk than creating value.

This increased complexity also has its impact on the public. One is now able to source medication over the internet and invest in financial schemes on the other side of the world in a matter of minutes. It is relatively straightforward to obtain information and to transact but it is increasingly more difficult to know how to use that information effectively and manage the risks that come with the activities at our disposal. Availability and choice also adds complexity to our decision-making, but makes professional judgement within an ethical framework ever more valuable.

At the heart of being a professional is the duty to uphold the public interest above one's own and to make accurate judgements based on acquired knowledge, skills, expertise and experience. This is knowledge that is regularly updated and skills that are regularly refreshed and developed. For accountants, the independent exercise of judgement, based around ethical values and technical skills, is the key to their future role in society. This is supported by our approach to professional work experience, which seeks to ensure that trainee accountants have exposure and an opportunity to learn from 'real life' dilemmas, while under supervision.

Today's professional accountant operates in an environment of time- and space-reducing technologies with an increased emphasis on ethics and corporate governance and demand for new, value-adding services. With greater automation and processing, the role of a professional accountant has evolved into one focused on managing uncertainty, complexity and strategic decision-making within an overall context of heightened governance. The attributes possessed by professional accountants facilitate entrepreneurship, help managers create value, manage risk and help us rationalise complexity. This is the role of the twenty-first-century professional.

Professionalism and accountancy

At the heart of being a professional accountant is the duty to serve the public interest. In the case of an accountant, this arguably goes beyond the financial. That is, the ethical duty of professional accountants extends into areas such as 'corporate social responsibility' and in trying to ensure that those they advise are aware of their own ethical responsibilities. This is exemplified in the core values of our professional body and in the ethical principles that not only shape and guide our behaviours but set the high expectations of us, as professionals. Our values of opportunity, diversity, accountability, innovation and integrity are deeply embedded in all aspects of what we do as a professional body. They are values that reflect our 'DNA' and determine our purpose.

Over 160 professional accountancy bodies representing 2.5 million accountants in 120 countries are members of the International Federation of Accountants (IFAC). ACCA has been instrumental in working with IFAC in developing the global standards on ethics, which are intended 'to assist member bodies to discharge their responsibilities to incorporate ethics education . . . so that candidates admitted to membership possess the professional values, ethics and attitudes required of professional accountants'.

ACCA's code of ethics and conduct reflects and amplifies the IFAC standard. Our members are guided by our fundamental principles of integrity, objectivity, professional competence and due care, confidentiality and professional behaviour, which must always be observed. Together, these principles identify and articulate what it means to be a professional accountant and express our commitment to the highest set of values. These principles, therefore, act as a benchmark against which members' behaviour is measured. They provide a framework that members can use to determine appropriate courses of action and offer independent judgements, whether as accountants employed in the public or private sectors, or offering their services to clients as a public practitioner.

ACCA is leading the agenda with regard to ensuring that the

professional accountant has the broad range of skills, values and behaviours that meet the changed expectations of business and society. Within ACCA's new syllabus, which is due to be launched in 2007, ethics and professional judgement is not only pervasive throughout but we have developed a new module entitled 'The professional accountant'. This module will be mandatory for all ACCA students. It aims to ensure that trainee accountants apply relevant knowledge and skills and exercise professional judgement in carrying out the role of the accountant relating to governance, internal control, compliance and the management of risk within an organisation, in the context of an overall ethical framework.

ACCA members and trainees understand that at the heart of every ethical dilemma lies a conflict of interest. With ever greater pressure to perform, they are aware of the conflicts of interest that can arise in trying to help their organisations and clients maximise profits. They understand the need to be sensitive as to when conflicts arise and the need to apply well-honed professional judgement to resolve them. As a professional body, we provide many support mechanisms for our members such as online courses, case studies, articles and a range of library resources.

Professionalism is critical to the operation and success of our global financial system. In presenting key financial and other strategic information, professional accountants are pillars of global capital markets and individual wealth. Professional accountants facilitate, monitor and lead the drive to ensure that an organisation's assets are used to the best interests of its stakeholders. Over 80 per cent of our members consider that promoting investors' confidence is vital. Investor confidence is achieved in a number of ways, for example through transparency in financial reporting, by championing corporate responsibility or by adhering to high professional and ethical standards.[2]

The heart of professionalism: professional judgement and ethics

Protection of the public can be achieved by ensuring that the fundamental values of professionalism are followed, supported by a rigorous regulatory framework. Our role as a professional body is to ensure that our members develop the ability to exercise independent professional judgement and to instil and promote our fundamental principles.

It is equally important that we do not over-regulate. Regulation needs to be proportionate to the risk and material consequences of misconduct. As previously discussed, part of the essence and value of professionals is their ability to exercise judgement based on ethical principles. Indeed, this is one of the key distinctions between professionals and non-professionals. To impose regulation disproportionate to risk would serve to constrain the use of judgement at the expense of the value professional accountants can bring to society. This is particularly pertinent as regulators sometimes seek to manage risk through simplification. That is, seeking to manage behaviours and decision-making by devising a set of rules which attempt to cover all conceivable scenarios and leave little room for professional judgement.

Professionals will face almost daily conflict from competing interests that could pose a threat to their professional values. Our qualification, continuing professional development (CPD) and member support services are aimed at ensuring that our members and students are well equipped to deal with these threats. While knowledge will assist with awareness of the threat, judgement will provide an understanding as to the options available in order to respond. However, ethical behaviour will ensure that the response is an appropriate one. Codes can only guide – it is individuals who decide. As a safety net for the public interest, ACCA, along with all the professional bodies, provides an independent disciplinary system for its members who breach standards.

A global concept of professionalism in accountancy

Globalisation and greater cross-border trade in services bring their own opportunities and challenges. The fusion of cultures and principles is giving rise to a common set of professional values and behaviours. With 370,000 members, affiliates and students located around the globe, ACCA is in a unique position with regard to setting common values of professionalism globally. Indeed, employers are attracted by the assurance of high standards across borders as a means of mitigating risk and also using the opportunities that come with global scale. We ensure consistency partly through adherence to educational and ethical guidelines set by IFAC and by having consistent approaches to our global offering of qualifications and CPD.

As a global organisation, ACCA passionately believes in diversity; hence our educational offerings are developed in consultation with members, employers, regulators and governments globally. The same standard of competence in a range of technical, management and personal skills is demanded from aspiring members, no matter the country in which they ultimately qualify. However, while the standards are consistent globally, the framework has been developed to be flexible enough for employers and individuals to tailor training.

As the professional class develops in the emerging economies of Asia, Central and Eastern Europe and Africa, ACCA recognises its role in facilitating that emergence by offering opportunities for several thousand individuals of ability to qualify as professional accountants to global standards. The diversity and mobility of our student and member base facilitates greater cross-cultural understanding and a shared body of experience and values that continue to build, develop and adapt to fit the global environment. As such we aim to promote the values of professionalism globally, even though in some developing markets there is little understanding of the differences between a degree and lifelong professional membership of a standards-based association.

Looking forward

Tomorrow's global professional accountant will face an ever-increasing set of competing values and complexity in the business environment. They will face ever-increasing demands from investors to improve financial returns and measure and report on forward-looking indicators. Given that financial markets survive and thrive on accurate and freely available information, the integrity of those who prepare that information is paramount. The ability to exercise judgement based on ethics will be the one constant that will ensure finance professionals maintain that integrity and successfully circumnavigate complexity and ethical dilemmas.

To ensure that accounting professionals remain the guardians of the public interest, continue to create value and facilitate entrepreneurship, ACCA calls on the profession, governments, regulators and investors to do the following:

O   Reassert what it means to be a professional and the values that professional accountants bring to our society through their involvement in every part of our economy.

O   Ensure that a profession providing variety, intellectual challenge and a high reputation is maintained in order to attract the best talent. This is critical to the future of our profession and its competitiveness. The accountancy profession should work together to maintain and raise standards globally.

O   Beware of the risk of 'de-professionalising' accountants. Avoid using blunt regulation at the expense of professional judgement, as this is unlikely to promote ethical behaviour. A black and white view of the world in which judgement is replaced by a 'rules-based' tick-box exercise counters the values of professionalism. The variety and instances of conflict are infinite. Attempts to anticipate and regulate for every eventuality are fruitless. Instead, focus on supporting professional bodies in ensuring that there is a high level of awareness and understanding of the principles that guide behaviours.

O   Promote the role of the accounting professional as the individual who can help businesses and individuals manage risk, simplify complexity, foster entrepreneurship and create value.

o   Maintain the values of professionalism and offer
    opportunities to people of ability and application. ACCA
    will continue to act on this. Indeed, part of our stated
    mission is 'to provide opportunity and access to people of
    ability around the world and to support our members
    throughout their careers in accounting, business and
    finance'.

ACCA will continue to strive for higher standards and to build a
global profession with increasing mobility, diversity and opportunity.
We will continue to represent and promote the profession globally
and aim to 'be the leading global professional accountancy body in
reputation, influence and size'. We invite our members, governments,
regulators, other accountancy professional bodies and investors to
join us in these commitments.

*Allan Blewitt is Chief Executive Officer of the Association of Chartered
Certified Accountants.*

Notes

1   Association of Chartered Certified Accountants, 'ACCA UK Survey by YouGov',
    2005 (unpublished).
2   Association of Chartered Certified Accountants, 'Responsibility: ACCA 100
    centenary survey', 2004, see www.acca100.com (accessed 26 May 2006).

11. Double devolution

How to put the amateurs in charge

Nick Aldridge and Astrid Kirchner

The third sector – Britain's charities and non-profit organisations – have built an enviable reputation for their ability to involve volunteers and citizens alongside professionals in building social capital and reforming public services. In taking on a more central role in local governance and service delivery, they will recast models of professionalism and accountability in the public and the third sector.

The major political parties aim to increase choice in public services by placing communities and individuals in control of the services they receive. Policy-making by government increasingly seeks to involve citizens directly through extensive consultation processes, such as the national and regional events held as part of 'Your Health, Your Care, Your Say'. Meanwhile, the Future Services Network, which has grown out of an alliance between acevo (Association of Chief Executives of Voluntary Organisations), the CBI (Confederation of British Industry) and the National Consumer Council, provides a cross-sectoral vehicle for exploring the complexities of the agenda from a provider perspective.

In a report last year,[1] it was argued that third sector organisations provide an ideal vehicle for such devolution of power. At their best, third sector organisations have compelling advantages in public service provision. They focus on service users rather than institutions, and have the flexibility to innovate and work across service silos.

And most compellingly for a government seeking to empower

communities, third sector organisations build social capital and inclusion through volunteering, while independent governance facilitates direct accountability to the communities they serve. Through community ownership, where service users may act as members or even trustees of organisations, third sector organisations can cement their local obligations. Nearly one million citizens now act as charity trustees.

Devolving power to communities will pose significant challenges for both government and the third sector, and particularly for the professionals and volunteers operating on the dividing line.

First, the third sector will need to become less wary of professionalism, demonstrating genuine accountability through sound governance, and developing its own capacity to deliver, without comprising the independence, drive, freedom and flexibility that characterise the sector.

Second, the role of public bodies, and particularly local government, must be refined and reformed within this new framework. Local authorities will need to embrace a more strategic role in assessing need, commissioning intelligently and guaranteeing quality – devolving power while holding its recipients to account.

Professionalism has long been a guilty secret in the third sector. Of course, the largest service-providing charities, from the Red Cross through to CfBT (the Centre for British Teachers), routinely employ thousands of professional staff, including doctors, nurses and teachers, in addition to the many accountants and lawyers that are needed to negotiate the pitfalls of charity law and finance. As a whole, the third sector now employs the full-time equivalent of over 1.5 million paid staff, with a turnover of £46 billion.[2]

Yet an ambivalent attitude to training and professional development pervades the sector. Leadership skills are essential in developing modern, enterprising and effective organisations, but have suffered from low prioritisation and chronic underspend on professional development within the sector. At present, training budgets in the third sector average only 1 per cent of turnover, compared with almost 3 per cent in the public and private sectors.[3] Only one in five organisations makes specific provision for developing its chief executive.[4]

Low spend results partly from the failure of third sector organisations to make the case for investment in internal infrastructure. Charities have done too little to dispel the public's distinction between funds that 'go to the cause', and those that are allegedly 'wasted on overheads'. Such a distinction is often simplistic and arbitrary: an extremely high telephone bill should be forgiven if incurred by the Samaritans. Moreover, guilt about paying competitive salaries for senior managers remains endemic in the sector. In an era of declining public deference and often unfocused demands for greater accountability, a culture that discourages investment in skills and professionalism will prove counterproductive and inefficient in the long term. Initiatives such as the ImpACT Coalition, which aims to increase charities' accountability and transparency, and the public-facing website 'Charity Facts', have begun to address the deficit in public understanding.[5]

Charities' culture of internal underinvestment has already led to a lack of demand for, and supply of, high-level training and development to address the needs of people operating in a very complex environment. The resulting skills gap in organisations causes underperformance (see figure 1). A more positive picture is slowly emerging as the sector begins to remedy the situation. The large business schools, including Cranfield, Ashridge and Cass, have now tailored programmes to the specific needs of third sector managers. The first qualification to be granted by acevo for third sector chief executives, accredited by the Institute of Directors, was launched in 2004. The third sector Leadership Centre, funded by the Home Office's ChangeUp investment programme, aims to plug other gaps in capacity.

The unique strength of many third sector organisations resides in their ability to involve unpaid volunteers alongside professional staff. Organisations such as Women's Royal Voluntary Service and British Trust for Conservation Volunteers aim to provide a professional,

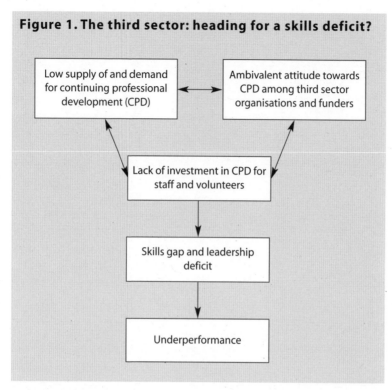

Figure 1. The third sector: heading for a skills deficit?

structured framework for supervising the work of volunteers for the public benefit. At its best, the flexible, creative and enthusiastic culture created by this mix of professionals and volunteers resembles the networks explored in recent work by Demos.[6]

Fascinating examples of a 'pro-am' culture of people pursuing amateur activities to professional standards also exist on a smaller scale. The Medical Engineering Resource Unit, a small charity that designs and manufactures bespoke equipment for disabled children and young people, engages 11 volunteer engineers alongside five professionals in its workshops. Last year it invented the 'e-bug', a small, powered, indoor wheelchair for disabled children aged as young as 12 months.

A blended culture of professionals and volunteers creates managerial and strategic complexities. Baroness Neuberger, who heads the Commission on the Future of Volunteering, has highlighted a risk that volunteering may become a way of 'offering public services on the cheap'.[7] It can be difficult to separate the components of a third sector service properly funded by the state, and delivered by paid staff, from the additional services provided by volunteers or funded by philanthropic donations. Charities such as Leonard Cheshire and Sue Ryder Care have undertaken major organisational reforms and campaigns to ensure that government will meet the full cost of all, and only, the public services they provide. And the government itself set a deadline of April 2006, now missed, for doing so.[8]

In an increasingly risk-averse culture, volunteering itself has been forced to professionalise. To safeguard young people, the volunteers who lead groups such as scout troops and those who work with young people must submit to Criminal Records Bureau checks alongside professional staff. The increased risks surrounding personal liability incurred through volunteering have led to an explosion in associated bureaucracy and insurance costs, prompting the Home Office to set up a task force on the issue in 2004. Volunteers make their contributions for a variety of reasons, so leading, managing and motivating volunteers requires managers to exercise leadership skills alongside considerable managerial competence. Volunteering England now offers an NOCN Level 3 qualification in managing volunteers. ASDAN even offers an accredited qualification for community volunteers themselves. See table 1 for more examples.

A similar tension between professionalism and voluntarism exists in the boards of third sector organisations. A long tradition of unpaid trusteeship is cherished by many in the sector, including the National Council for Voluntary Organisations, as a defining characteristic. However, boards may struggle to implement professional standards of board development and appraisal within this constraint, despite a sector-wide commitment to do so in its first *Code of Governance*,[9] published only last year. The trustees' association *Charity Trustee Networks* is more a support network than a development agency.

Table 1. A sample of courses and qualifications in the third sector

Provider	Name	Level	Website
acevo	Next Generation Chief Executives programme – delivered with Cass Business School	Those whose next role may be chief executive	www.acevo.org.uk
	New Chief Executives programme – delivered with Cass Business School	For recently appointed CEOs or people new to the sector	
	Institute of Directors/ acevo Diploma in company direction	For people interested in gaining chartered director status	
	Advanced leadership development programme – delivered with Ashridge Business School	CEOs who have been in post for a few years and are looking to refresh skills and revitalise working practices	
	Developing the experienced leader – delivered with Cranfield Business School	Experienced CEOs who are looking to further develop their leadership capabilities to enhance effectiveness of the organisation that they lead	
ASDAN	Level 1 & 2 Certificate in Community Volunteering	For volunteers	www.asdan. org.uk

Table 1. *continued*

Provider	Name	Level	Website
Cass Business School	MSc/PgDip in Voluntary Sector Management	The course is intended for highly motivated graduate-level staff with three or more years of management experience, and delivers immediate management benefits directly back into the organisation as well as providing valuable personal career development for the individual	www.cass.city. ac.uk/charity effectiveness/
Charity Training	Level 4 BTEC Professional Certificate in Voluntary Sector Management	It is anticipated that learners studying for the BTEC Professional Certificate in Voluntary Sector Management will either be preparing for a 'middle manager' role or already be in a similar role; route into MSc/ PgDip in Voluntary Sector Management for people with no prior academic qualification	www.charity training.com

Table 1. *continued*

Provider	Name	Level	Website
National Open College Network	NOCN Level 3 Award in Managing Volunteers, National Accreditation	Particularly suitable for those who are new to the responsibility of managing volunteers, are existing managers who do not have a qualification in this area or those who work in the sector and wish to progress to a managerial role	www.nocn.org.uk

While a culture of well-intentioned amateurism apparently lowers barriers to board membership, it results in skills deficits on boards, disguises underperformance and promotes poor recruitment practice. More than two-thirds of charities recruit their trustees by word of mouth, which often results in an evident lack of board diversity.

Uniquely in UK corporate governance, charity boards usually consist exclusively of unpaid non-executives, a legacy of charity law that derives from a need to uphold the probity of philanthropic trusts. An increasing number of organisations are now updating their governance structures through unitary boards, and including a minority of senior executives as trustees. Although 50 per cent of acevo members believe a unitary board model best suits their organisations, every change requires permission from the Charity Commission. Fewer than 5 per cent have thus far secured such permission.

Many third sector boards struggle to engage their members and service users directly in organisational governance. The proportion of members voting in professional associations' board elections is usually under 30 per cent and sometimes less than 10 per cent.[10] Many third sector organisations, including professional associations, empower service users by placing them directly on the board. They seek to remedy the skills shortages that may result through co-options, or by 'guiding' the democratic process. Increasingly, membership bodies are professionalising their governance structures, streamlining their boards and creating new advisory 'councils' to represent members and stakeholders.

Third sector organisations have found themselves at the sharp end of difficult questions concerning professionalism. Attempting to balance demands for greater accountability and better performance with a culture of inclusion and user-participation has led many to experiment with new structures of governance, and more rigorous standards of management, including volunteer management. These experiments represent a vital step in reversing the sector's historic underinvestment in its own infrastructure and development.

David Miliband MP, Secretary of State for the Environment, has noted that 'better health and education, lower crime, and environmental sustainability cannot be achieved without citizens' participation'. He looks to the third sector as 'the supplier of power to individuals and communities. . . . In its role providing advocacy for communities, it provides a voice for citizens.'[11]

The idea of 'double devolution', in which power is passed from central government to local authorities, then devolved further to citizens and communities, features strongly in new government policy. To succeed, double devolution should build on existing channels for active citizenship, and invest heavily in community capacity-building. Such an approach provides a golden opportunity to replicate third sector successes in involving citizens and service users in governance, service delivery and advocacy. As potential channels for double devolution, third sector organisations may thereby assume a more prominent role in local democracy.

Alongside the strengths of the third sector, the challenges they face in maintaining professionalism and accountability may reappear on a larger scale within a programme of double devolution. Local authorities question the competence and legitimacy of the community groups engaged in local advocacy. The Empty Homes Agency, which works to bring empty properties back into use, has had to make rapid assessments of the status and levels of community support of local action groups.

In turn, local third sector organisations struggle to negotiate the institutional bureaucracy integral to working partnerships with local government. Research by representatives of the local third sector has shown that most local organisations do not yet know where to find announcements of relevant funding opportunities by local authorities.[12] Uneasy compromises must be reached, and local inter-action exemplifies the challenges and ambiguities at play in partner-ship working between the state and independent organisations.

Such ambiguities will reach a crunch point in decisions on resource allocation. While public policy has begun to focus on the third sector's role in building and representing communities, funding for such roles is naturally dwarfed by spending on public service delivery. Meanwhile, the rigorous auditing measures employed by government watchdogs have led to a growing number of strings being attached to the public purse. Despite numerous deregulation initiatives, the sector continues to report burgeoning red tape. Conversely, sector policy-makers' oft-aired concerns about the potential loss of third sector independence would be tested spectacularly if far more public funding for community advocacy were placed on the table.

Similar challenges will apply to the parallel agenda, also shared by the three major parties, to give the third sector a more central role in public service delivery. The government's recent action plan[13] outlined concrete measures to scale up this role, building the sector into a significant provider from a starting point of less than 2 per cent of public expenditure.[14] In public services, as in local governance, the best third sector organisations will attempt to reshape policy priorities around the needs of citizens and communities, rather than around budget headings and institutions.

In forging partnerships, third sector organisations will need to convince local authorities that they have the will and capacity to combine professionalism, accountability and strong leadership with community ownership and an ability to engage the elusive 'grass roots'. Local officials and politicians will need to embrace a more detached, regulatory role as commissioners and convenors of local services, not necessarily as their providers.

Commissioning must become more flexible, more strategic and more needs-based. While some services might be co-produced by local communities, other, specialised and highly valuable third sector services achieve critical mass only at regional or even national level. The structures to make such decisions rapidly and responsively are not yet in place.

Above all, both sides will be invited to innovate and embrace major risks, which will prove counterintuitive both to trustees and to senior officials. Future regulatory frameworks, and mechanisms of accountability for performance, must be stretched to recognise and support this new requirement.

The governance and management of third sector organisations is in flux, oscillating between increasing demands for professionalism and accountability, and the need to increase diversity, engage citizens and reduce barriers to entry for stakeholders. Organisations themselves have found creative solutions to this dilemma, developing advisory councils and networks of users to sit alongside conventional governance structures, and professionalising volunteer management with a view to making volunteering easier, safer and more rewarding.

A double devolution agenda, setting out to hand power from local government down to communities and citizens, will thrust third sector organisations into the spotlight as potential gatekeepers to community involvement. To stand up under scrutiny, the models they employ for involving volunteers alongside professionals must be robust and fit for purpose. If it passes muster, the third sector's evolving conception of professionalism and accountability will become ever more influential in shaping public policy.

Nick Aldridge is Director of Strategy and Astrid Kirchner is Head of Professional Development at acevo.

Notes

1   N Aldridge, *Communities in Control* (London: Social Market Foundation, 2005).
2   J Kendall, *The Voluntary Sector* (London: LSE, 2004).
3   Voluntary Sector National Training Organisation, *Futureskills* (London: VSNTO, 2003).
4   acevo, *Making a Difference: Remuneration survey* (London: acevo, 2005).
5   See especially www.charityfacts.org/charity_facts/charity_costs/index.html (accessed 14 May 2006).
6   C Leadbeater and P Miller, *The Pro-Am Revolution* (London: Demos, 2004).
7   J Neuberger 'Don't take volunteers for granted' (an edited version of speech delivered at the launch of The Commission on the Future of Volunteering), *Guardian*, 29 Mar 2006, see http://society.guardian.co.uk/futureforpublicservices/comment/0,,1742163,00.html (accessed 14 May 2006).
8   See www.fullcostrecovery.org.uk (accessed 14 May 2006).
9   *A Code of Governance for the Voluntary and Community Sector* (London: acevo, CTN, ICSA and NCVO, 2005).
10   B Taylor, S Lee and N Aldridge, *Leading the Professions* (London/Henley-on-Thames: acevo and Henley Management College, 2005).
11   D Miliband, 'Putting people in control', keynote speech at NCVO conference, London, 21 Feb 2006.
12   Research by National Council of Associations for Voluntary Service, London, 2006 (unpublished).
13   Publication forthcoming.
14   NCVO, *Voluntary Sector Almanac* (London: NCVO, 2006).

12. Professionals in partnership

Laura Empson

In recent years, management writers have held up professional partnerships as operational exemplars for the knowledge economy. They are supposedly characterised by strong but informal learning cultures, dedication to client service and high levels of personal autonomy. Partnerships, it is argued, provide the ideal way to marry personal freedom and opportunity with mutual trust and collaboration among knowledge workers.

Ironically, while companies in manufacturing and retail are being told that they should emulate professional partnerships, many accountants, consultants and lawyers are taking up their management practices. In their struggle to compete, growing numbers of professional service firms are abandoning the traditional legal form and management practices of partnership, introducing corporate-style structures and systems.

The concepts of partnership and professionalism have been inextricably connected for as long as professionals have worked together. The danger, therefore, is that in abandoning one, professionals risk jeopardising the other. For example, commentators have suggested that the need to satisfy external shareholders will undermine professional ethos.

However, professionalism is not simply being colonised by corporate interests. Partnership is most fundamentally a state of mind not a legal form and managers can do a great deal to ensure that it survives and thrives in a changing world.[1] Where they do, the partnership ethos has the vital capacity to hold the worst excesses of corporatism in check. But first, why does it work and what is threatening it?

Managing professionals

The partnership form of governance is particularly suited to the distinctive nature of professional work. Professional service firms[2] apply specialist technical knowledge to create customised solutions for clients. In order to customise in this way, professionals must be free to exercise their autonomy and independent judgement.

However, the desire for autonomy may go further than this. Professionals seek opportunities to pursue personal fulfilment by taking on assignments that they find intellectually rewarding, or that satisfy their creative or altruistic impulses. Maximising income is not necessarily a professional's primary objective – traditionally a source of reassurance to clients and a basis for the professions' claims to privileged regulatory status.

Traditionally, partnership has been seen as the best way to deliver the degree of autonomy and self-actualisation that professionals require. In a partnership, an elite group of senior professionals combine the roles of owners, managers and core producers. As owners they share both the profits of the firm and unlimited personal liability for each other's actions. These features are designed to ensure that partners' self-interest is tempered by mutual trust and collaboration. Typically, partners retain the right to vote on key management decisions and to elect representatives from among their ranks to perform senior management roles on a fixed-term basis. Within this context, professionals may have considerable scope to pursue personal fulfilment while also taking account of commercial imperatives.

Declining incidence of professional partnerships

Until 20 years ago, partnership was the pre-eminent form of governance in most professional sectors. Within the established professions, such as law and accounting, partnership was viewed traditionally as the only legitimate model of organisation. Firms within aspiring professions, such as consulting and investment banking, often chose to organise themselves as partnerships, thus assuming the mantle of professionalism that partnership conveyed.

In the 1980s everything began to change. The Big Bang in 1986 wiped out most of the stockbroking partnerships in the City of London, and the flotation of Goldman Sachs in 1998 signalled the end of an era in investment banking. By the start of the twenty-first century, 32 of the 50 largest consulting firms in the world were publicly quoted. Of the remainder, only eight remained partnerships, approximately half the number of ten years previously. Recently, accounting firms have sought to separate and incorporate their non-audit activities (the regulatory regime in many countries still requires auditors to remain partnerships). As a result, almost 50 per cent of the world's top 100 accounting firms are now organised as privately held or publicly quoted corporations.

Law firms have been slower to change than other professional service firms. Although UK law firms have been permitted to incorporate since 1992, relatively few have exercised this option. However, since 2001, they have been permitted to adopt limited liability partnership (LLP) status and many have now converted. The Clementi Review of 2004,[3] which recommended the lifting of restrictions on the ownership of law firms, means that in future it will be possible for UK law firms to be acquired by publicly quoted companies and to go public themselves.

Why the decline?

In a sense, partnership has been a victim of its own success, which has brought new pressures to bear on forms of governance.

First, high profits and growth rates in recent years, which have seen firms straddle numerous services and countries, have themselves pressured collective decision-making and mutual monitoring. As they have grown, professional service firms have adopted corporate methods of hierarchical and bureaucratic control. The largest accounting firms, for example (which were the first professional partnerships with more than 1,000 partners), long ago ceased to rely on consensus-based decision-making for major firm-wide issues.

A second factor leading to the flight from partnership is the increasing demand for capital, which partnerships find it difficult to raise. By the mid-1980s, investment banks found themselves struggling to fund their increasingly sophisticated information technology (IT) requirements and to meet the rapidly rising capital demands of their underwriting and trading activities. During the 1990s, the need to invest in IT had spread across professional service firms, particularly in the consulting sector.

Growth and the need for capital are not the only factors that have led increasing numbers of professional service firms towards incorporation. The dramatic increase in litigation in recent years has prompted many partnerships to convert to LLP status in order to avoid the crippling costs of partner indemnity insurance. At the same time, the commoditisation of knowledge and expertise means that there is less of a need to secure professionals' cooperation by offering them a share of ownership and a say in the management of the firm. In addition, changing work trends have seen growing numbers of junior professionals choosing roles where they can acquire money and status quickly, turning away from partnership as they observe the extraordinary pressures under which partners in large and successful professional service firms now operate.

So what makes partnership so special and does it still work in the modern competitive context? Through a UK government-funded research study of the legal, accounting and consulting professions,[4] I have sought to understand the special nature of partnership, how it is created and sustained, and how it can adapt to survive and thrive in a changing world.

Partnership ethos

The special nature of a partnership is that you've got a commitment and buy-in that is so special. . . . You have these amazing people who really feel they can sort of take on the world and feel part of a club, a very, very, very special club. And I think in a way that's really what partnership means to me. . . . It's quite a personal and emotional thing.

Practice head, law firm

People here are generally doing things in the best interests of the firm as a whole. In a corporation, you hear stories emerging about how people can get ahead by doing other people down. It's that kind of internal competition, cynical behaviour, that we do not experience in the partnership.

Partner, consulting firm

These professionals make it clear that, far more than a legal form of governance, partnership is an ethos – a shared set of beliefs and behaviours. The two legal features of collective ownership and unlimited personal liability represent the foundations on which the partnership ethos is constructed. As owners of the firm, partners have a clear imperative to maximise their individual autonomy. They are, after all, effectively shareholders and what is the point of a firm if it is not to serve the interests of its shareholders? This individualistic impulse is tempered by unlimited personal liability, which binds all partners together by making them individually liable for the actions of their colleagues. Partners, therefore, have a clear financial imperative to operate collectively, to monitor and support each other, both at a personal and professional level.

This tension between individualism and collectivism is fundamental to understanding the special nature of partnership. The legal form of partnership creates the tension – the ethos of partnership resolves that tension. Typically, in those firms with a strong partnership ethos, it represents a powerful unifying force among the partners which serves to counteract the self-serving impulses that drive each partner individually. In firms with long-serving partners, this sense of collectivism is often associated with strong personal relationships.

Can a corporation imitate a partnership?

Recognising the partnership ethos as distinct from partnership as a legal construct opens up interesting possibilities. It suggests that publicly quoted corporations potentially can embody the most meaningful and valuable aspects of the partnership ethos while avoiding the legal trappings of partnership. Just as a partnership ethos resolves the tensions created by the legal form of partnership, so it may be able to resolve those created by that of the corporation.

Some corporations have deliberately set out to imitate aspects of partnership, creating the feel of partnership within a corporate form. McKinsey & Company, for example, incorporated in the 1950s. However, to the outside world and to the consultants within it, the firm still embodies many of the best qualities of a partnership. As Marvin Bower (managing director 1950–67 and described as 'the soul of McKinsey') says: 'We find it takes intensive and continuous effort to preserve the real and useful partnership spirit.'[5] McKinsey does not rely purely on preserving the spirit of partnership, but also seeks to mimic the structure of partnership. For example, the managing director is elected by 270 of the most senior 'partners'. The term 'partner' is still used informally because 'even though it may not be legally accurate it can bring out some of the best qualities in people'.[6] While such claims should be treated with caution, McKinsey is trying to hold on to something it deems commercially valuable – its ethos.

McKinsey is a corporation but, like a partnership, it lacks external shareholders. My own research into professional service firms supports the idea that it is possible to create and sustain elements of the partnership ethos within a publicly quoted corporation, as well as a privately owned one. But it is not easy. For the process to be effective, professionals and their managers must be strongly committed to the partnership ethos and work actively to create and sustain it.

Creating and sustaining the partnership ethos

While the partnership ethos is clearly associated with partnership as a legal form, my research suggests it is not explained by it.[7] In the partnerships that I studied, I found that three fundamental elements help to create and sustain the partnership ethos: the structures, the systems and the socialisation processes with which the legal form is typically associated.

Within partnership, *socialisation* is the protracted process by which an individual is prepared to join the society of partners. During socialisation, a professional develops the requisite skills to make partner, demonstrating that they can behave with authority towards clients, make good decisions and be trusted by the partnership as a whole.

This process is fundamental to creating and sustaining the partnership ethos, which requires the interests of the individual to be reconciled with those of the collective. Through socialisation, the professional internalises an extensive set of norms that enables them, in effect, to become self-regulating. Potential partners learn to subsume their own identity into that of the profession, the organisation and, ultimately, the partner group. A partner in an accounting firm explained to me:

> *As a partner I have a huge amount of personal independence. No one tells me what to do. . . . I do what I want, but the things I want are likely to help the firm because that is the way I have been trained. At one level we are completely independent, but we all march to the same tune without even thinking about it.*
>
> Partner, accounting firm

Once a professional makes partner, the *systems* for evaluating, rewarding and sanctioning partners are fundamental to creating and sustaining the partnership ethos. The innate drive of most professionals, together with their sense of commitment to the partnership, ensures that they continue to generate and maximise profits on behalf of the firm. However, if an individual's commitment fails, sanctions tend to be subtle in the first instance. Partners signal their displeasure in the same way that school children marginalise and ostracise their peers who do not conform to their norms of behaviour. A partner I interviewed in a major global law firm recalled somewhat nostalgically:

> *When we were a smaller firm you could get rid of partners by saying – 'You've lost the confidence of your peers old boy. You either piss off now and we'll give you a year's money and be nice to you, or you can stay and we'll make it bloody uncomfortable for you.' . . . It isn't so simple nowadays.*
>
> Partner, law firm

As professional service firms grow and their partner group becomes less stable and more heterogeneous, informal methods of partner management are less effective, and more formalised systems of evaluation and sanction become necessary. This change begins to compromise the professionals' traditional expectation of high levels of personal autonomy.

The third fundamental element which helps to create and sustain the partnership ethos is the management *structure*. The nature of managerial authority can be highly contingent, even in a large partnership. One practice head explained to me:

> *I am responsible for a large group of partners, all of whom are very bright, at least as bright as I am, all of whom have big egos, all of whom are owners of the business with as much right to vote and draw profits as I have. The process of being in charge or leading is about building consensus – it's not easy because most people are attracted to this business because they are independent, they like doing their own thing. Essentially they want to be left alone until it's something that kind of connects them and then it's – 'why wasn't I consulted?'*
>
> Practice head, law firm

Looking to the future

A partnership ethos has the potential to resolve the tensions implicit in the corporate form of governance, just as it has done with those created by partnership governance. As partnerships grow large, it is inevitable that governance structures will evolve, requiring partners to delegate authority to a select group to manage the firm on their behalf. This is a necessary precondition for growth. However, even as a firm dispenses with partnership as a form of governance, managers can sustain a partnership ethos if they draw on a deep understanding of their firm and focus on the threats it may face. If they do so, some of the worst elements of corporate management structures – a single-minded focus on profit combined with lack of care for the public good and loss of collegiality – can be held in check by retaining and developing socialisation processes, partner management systems and governance structures that support and sustain the partnership ethos. Partnership can remain a key element of professionalism, and as an ethos rather than a legal form it can nevertheless continue to serve as a regulator of firms' activities and as a source of reassurance for their clients.

Laura Empson is Director of the Clifford Chance Centre for the Management of Professional Service Firms at Saïd Business School, Oxford University (www.sbs.ox.ac.uk/ccc).

Notes

1   For a more comprehensive analysis of this issue see L Empson, 'Surviving and thriving in a changing world: the special nature of partnership' in L Empson (ed), *Managing the Modern Law Firm* (Oxford: Oxford University Press, Jan 2007, forthcoming). Contact laura.empson@sbs.ox.ac.uk for further details.

2   For a more detailed definition of professional service firms and an overview of the relevant research literature see www.sbs.ox.ac.uk/ccc (accessed 16 May 2006).

3   D Clementi, 'Review of the regulatory framework for legal services in England and Wales: final report' (Dec 2004).

4   L Empson and C Chapman, 'Consequences of changing forms of governance for the management of professional service firms', Economic and Social Research Council of Great Britain (RES-000-22-0204), 2003.

5   M Bower, *Will to Lead: Running a business with a network of leaders* (Boston, MA: Harvard Business School Press, 1997).

6   Ibid.

7   See Empson, 'Surviving and thriving in a changing world'.

13. Overly controlled or out of control?

Management consultants and the new corporate professionalism

Matthias Kipping, Ian Kirkpatrick and Daniel Muzio

Introduction

Knowledge-intensive occupations and organisations have recently emerged as 'hot topics' attracting considerable academic literature and commercial interest. In this context, management and systems consultants have enjoyed a particularly 'explosive' growth record. During the last two decades of the twentieth century, the worldwide market for consulting services increased between 10 and 15 per cent per year, considerably more than the global economy.[1] In 2003 the total revenue of the top ten consulting firms stood at over $51 billion,[2] while, according to one recent estimate, the workforce of the top 30 management consulting firms worldwide rose from just over 100,000 in 1995 to 450,000 in 2003. Growth in this business has, therefore, coincided with the creation of some mega-firms with many thousands of consultants – in a sector traditionally, and still, dominated by small- and medium-sized consultancies.

This growth in the market for business advice is assumed to have marked implications for the way expert groups such as management consultants organise themselves. Unlike the more established professions, such as law, accountancy, medicine and architecture, they have not relied very much, if at all, on the occupational closure regimes. Nor do they share the same concern with accreditation and regulation. One reason given for this is that the knowledge base of these groups is too esoteric, fragmented and perishable to be formalised into a traditional sense (as easily recognisable 'professional' credentials).[3] Another is that they no longer need or aspire to have professional status. Management consultants, we are told, prefer to organise through loose networks, are more entrepreneurial and able to pursue their interests through the open market. As such their emerging form of organisation is quite different from that of traditional professions and, for some observers, represents an alternative paradigm to it.

These developments are frequently celebrated by the media and are widely endorsed by academics and policy-makers. Indeed, the notions of knowledge work and a knowledge-based economy would seem to have considerable appeal, conjuring up images of 'smart people, in smart jobs, doing smart things in smart ways, for smart money'.[4] For the employee, the implication is that work has become increasingly rewarding, varied and challenging. According to Alvesson, workers in the new knowledge-intensive firms 'typically operate very autonomously and rely on their own judgement and authority', while managers 'find themselves operating like diplomats – always engaged in negotiations and trying to find compromises'.[5] The consumer and wider public are also said to benefit. Knowledge-based occupations are credited with the discovery of new innovative types of knowledge, which are somehow revitalising the whole economy in a bottom-up process. Public and private sector organisations increasingly rely on external sources of organisational and managerial innovation, which – so the story goes – enables them to react faster, more flexibly, and possibly more economically to changes in their environment.

In this essay our aim is to develop a different account of these complex changes. We suggest that the main reason management consultants have failed to professionalise is not so much their fragmented knowledge base and differing aspirations, but because large firms in this sector have sought to resist and stifle such change. The dominant trend, we suggest, is towards a form of *corporate professionalism* in which organisations themselves become the main locus of professional exercise, closure and regulation. One outcome of this is that the organisation of these firms has become increasingly bureaucratic, a far cry from the upbeat image of empowered knowledge workers. As for consumers, we will show that consultants have developed a number of proxies, some of them of a purely symbolic nature, to signal quality to their clients. We also show – namely by contrasting the fate of Andersen and McKinsey in the Enron case – that these are not sufficient to ensure quality of service and neither is the reputation of a particular service provider.

The evolution of management consulting: professionalism without a profession

The consulting business is very broad and varied with shifts in products over time since the early part of the twentieth century.[6] The global nature of this business means that from an early stage there have been few barriers to entry into national markets or from firms and professions operating in other sectors (most recently from IT). For these reasons management consulting evolved in a way quite different from more regulated professional sectors such as law or accounting. While in the latter there has been relative stability of firms and modes of regulation, the consultancy business has developed in a series of waves. Each wave was associated with different types of products and markets – and the rise to dominance of different firms – some of them new entrants, others previously operating in niche markets. The dominant consultancies in the first wave, dominant from the 1930s to the 1950s, provided services related to the 'scientific' organisation of individual work and the productive process in factories and offices. By contrast, the most visible consultancies in the second wave, which dominated the industry from the 1960s to 1980s, concentrated on advice to top management in terms of corporate strategy and structure. Finally, those in the – still emerging – third wave focus on the use of information and communication technologies to control far-flung and extensively networked client organisations.

These waves can be explained both as a consequence of changes in the environment and the activities of consultants themselves. Changes in the predominant types of client organisation and the attention of senior management provided opportunities for consultancies to offer different types of services. This situation was in turn exploited by different groups of professionals, or what are sometimes referred to as 'institutional entrepreneurs'.[7] Thus, in the second strategy and organisation wave, consultancies like McKinsey took advantage from the rise of MBAs to general management positions. The third wave is somewhat different in that the IT-based consultancies sell the knowledge provided by the firm as a whole, rather than relying on the qualifications of the individual consultants. These firms have been able to respond to (and partly shape) broader processes of restructuring and outsourcing in large corporations and in public services.

According to Kipping,[8] once the dominant service providers had become established they found it difficult to respond to subsequent changes, because their reputation was linked to other kinds of services and neither the skills of their consulting staff nor their cost structure were adequate. Those firms taking advantage of these opportunities were either new entrants or – probably more often – had operated in related markets before, but now grew rapidly. They eventually came to dominate the market and public perception, while the previously dominant firms gradually declined, were bought up or disappeared entirely. Since client types and needs did not change overnight, all of these developments occurred rather slowly. The result was that quite different types of consulting firms co-existed for prolonged periods of time.

The pattern of change outlined above generated very special problems for management consultants to develop a strong professional identity. An obvious difficulty was that the knowledge base itself was constantly changing as new forms entered the market, innovating with new products and ways of working. In many ways, management consulting was and remains a contested terrain, hard to pin down and formalise. But while important, this kind of obstacle to professional formation should not be overstated. Doing so may lead us to neglect how, under the appropriate circumstances, occupations with fragmented knowledge bases have indeed managed to professionalise. One example of this might be engineering (or even accounting), which is articulated around a cluster of specialisations somehow connected by some common foundational principles. Also, focusing just on the knowledge dimension may lead us to ignore other explanations for the failure to professionalise. In particular it may obscure from view the activities of large firms themselves in seeking to oppose such change and their attempts to define professionalism differently to suit their own business and labour market requirements.

To illustrate this last point it is useful to look more closely at changes within one country: the UK. Here the initial phase of development of the consulting business, from the mid-1950s, did see moves to establish common standards for consulting work and accreditation. This led to the establishment of peak organisations such as the Management Consultancies Association (MCA), a body representing employers, and the Institute of Management Consultants (IMC) to accredit and later register individual practitioners.[9] By the early 1960s, consultants were well on their way to establishing an independent professional organisation and some degree of labour market closure. However, from the late 1960s these attempts to organise were undermined by the increasing dominance of US-based strategy firms in the UK, such as McKinsey and Company or Booz-Allen & Hamilton. Rather than relying on industry-wide associations, these firms drew their 'professional' status from their own practices, imitating law firms, and actively worked against efforts to extend certification.[10]

More recently this pattern has been extended. As we have seen, since the mid-1990s a different group of firms have dominated the industry, some of which come from accounting (Accenture) and others providing mainly IT-based services (IBM). Like the earlier wave of strategy firms these organisations also sought to resist attempts to develop a strong independent profession. The focus instead was on building their own brand through massive advertising and sponsorship efforts, and assuming full control over the selection and training of new consultants – which the strategy firms had partially 'subcontracted' to leading business schools. This in turn has had an impact on the strategies pursed by the IMC, leading it closer to an organisational model of professionalisation, whereby the institute is increasingly seeking to admit into membership and regulate entire organisations as well as individual consultants.

What this brief history suggests is that, in the UK context at least, the professionalisation project of consultants failed not so much because of the ambiguity of such work (although this was important to a certain extent), but because of the resistance of the large firms that dominated the sector. These firms, at least initially, were interested in 'professionalism' as a means of enhancing their brand or reputational capital. Importantly, however, this interest did not extend to independent professional regulation itself. Increasingly the large organisation became the main locus of professional exercise, closure and regulation, shaping the development and behaviour of the sector field and determining the status and material conditions of practitioners.

Corporate professionalism and the consultant: from brainwork to procedure

The trend towards 'corporate professionalism' outlined above has had important implications for the work experience of consultants. Earlier we noted that a dominant assumption shared by academics and the media is that management consultants tend to work in firms that 'deviate heavily from bureaucratic principles'.[11] Such firms are decentralised with limited reliance on formal hierarchy and 'relatively few formal procedures to standardize and share knowledge'.[12] But while numerous examples of this mode of working can be found, most indications are that the large firms that dominate the market today do not operate in this way. On the contrary, the trend may be towards a more regulated and controlled form of consulting than was the norm even 15 or 20 years ago.

In terms of governance there has been a marked shift towards the model of a publicly owned corporation. Of the 50 largest consulting firms worldwide between 1989 and 2001, the number of publicly owned firms rose from five to 31, while the number of partnerships declined.[13] A more bureaucratic approach is also apparent in the leverage ratios of these firms – the proportion of senior consultants to junior staff. At Andersen Consulting (now Accenture) 'there are more than 30 consultants for each partner', compared with a ratio in McKinsey of seven to one.[14] Because of this individual consultants often have limited freedom when it comes to execution, but must work according to detailed guidelines that state how to carry out different kinds of assignments step-by-step. Such guidelines, in turn, were usually based on the experiences drawn from previous projects, codified through elaborate knowledge management systems and then stored in powerful databases accessible by all members of the consultancy.

The push to standardise and control the work of individual consultants is also reflected in the way human resources are managed. In the larger firms a primary focus of recruitment is no longer on qualified professionals, but on university undergraduates, sometimes specialised in the IT area. Indeed, the emphasis now seems to be on 'recruiting *potential* management consultants rather than proven consultants'.[15] Because of this, many firms invest heavily in selection and internal training. Some have also developed elaborate systems to familiarise new recruits with the consultancy's methodologies, procedure protocols and ubiquitous knowledge management system.[16] All this is a far cry from the popular image of a highly independent, mobile, knowledge workforce able to bargain special privileges from employers. Rather, as David Craig suggests: 'The world's major management consultancies have become enormous factories churning out thousands of almost identical "vanilla" consultants, whose time must be sold to clients, whether clients have problems to be solved or not.'[17]

Corporate professionalism and the client: is reputation really enough?

The reluctance of the large consulting firms to submit to a professional regime also has implications for clients, leaving them without any form of external quality control. Consulting is a typical 'experience good'. Due to its intangible nature and the involvement of the client organisation, its quality can be assessed only during and after the project.[18] In the other professions, the resulting uncertainty and risk has been reduced through entry barriers and quality control mechanisms imposed by the professional association, which also enforces these standards (since for the member firms exclusion from the association would normally mean exclusion from the market). By contrast, when hiring a consulting firm, clients take significant risks and if something goes wrong can pursue the firm only through the normal justice system.

Of course many would argue that reputation is sufficient to help regulate the market and prevent possible abuses.[19] Consultants have, historically, gone to considerable lengths to develop proxies to signal quality to their potential clients and possible third parties. Firms in the second wave, and in particular McKinsey, did this largely by mimicking an existing profession, law. Marvin Bower, who was the driving force behind the transformation of McKinsey from an expert to a professional consulting firm, had himself worked in a law firm before. This experience apparently convinced him that in order to 'improve their standing [...] consultants should emulate the older, or classical, professions by adopting and enforcing self-imposed standards of competence, ethics, responsibility, and independence'.[20] Mimicry went down to the detail of behaviour and appearances – which in turn inspired consultants elsewhere to imitate the 'McKinsey look of successful young professionals, which apparently included a Porsche sports car, a house in a fashionable suburb, skiing as the favourite sport and regular visits to art galleries'.[21] And once it started hiring recent MBA graduates instead of experienced businessmen, the consultancy adopted a 'tough' selection process, involving several rounds of 'gruelling' interviews to demonstrate to potential clients that only the best would work for them.[22]

The dominant firms of today, such as Accenture and IBM, use different strategies to demonstrate quality, partly because they have more financial resources, partly because they no longer feel obliged to maintain the semblance of professionalism. Thus, many of the large consultancies are running major advertising campaigns. Accenture, for example, has been using Tiger Woods in both television and print ads, building its message on a play with his name: 'Go on. Be a Tiger.' Many firms have also been developing extensive knowledge management systems. These represent an additional way of enhancing reputation and brand image, persuading clients that a firm has at its disposal systematic and hi-tech ways of dealing with their problems.

Notwithstanding these efforts, one must question how far reputation and brand image are sufficiently robust mechanisms for ensuring quality and protecting clients. There is growing evidence that consultants have given flawed advice without being punished for it.[23] In the UK it is estimated that ongoing efforts to computerise the NHS may now cost £30 billion, five times the projected cost, while £450 million was spent on a system for the Child Support Agency that does not work.[24] But perhaps the most widely publicised example of such failure is Enron. Everybody shared in the praise for this exceptional company and its visionary 'asset light' business strategy, not least McKinsey and Co. After all, Jeff Skilling was a former director of the consultancy and McKinsey had projects at Enron almost without interruption. In its publications the consultancy heaped praise on its star client: 'Few companies will be able to achieve the excitement extravaganza that Enron has in its remarkable business transformation, but many could apply some of the principles.'[25]

Given this strong association between Enron and McKinsey it is perhaps all the more surprising that when Enron did collapse everybody got the blame *except for* the consultants. Arthur Andersen, Enron's accountants and auditors, also had supplied some consulting services, but that was not the reason it eventually disappeared as a firm. It was because Arthur Andersen was alleged to have broken its legal and professional obligations that it was barred from auditing publicly quoted companies, which drove the firm out of business. As for McKinsey, it got some bad press. An article in *Business Week* by John Byrne highlighted the fact that Enron was only the last of a whole string of McKinsey clients to declare bankruptcy.[26] Others included K-Mart, Global Crossing and Swissair. But this caused only a small dent in the consultancy's reputation and it was soon back to business as usual.

Conclusions

A key assertion of this essay is that knowledge-based occupations such as management consultancy are at the forefront of the development of a new corporate form of professionalism. This recognises how under present historical conditions, traditional patterns of collective organisation based on formal credentials and individual accreditation may not be sustainable. Such strategies have effectively served the occupational ambitions of the more established professions, such as law, accountancy and medicine. However, a consultant's knowledge is more indeterminate and less amenable to certification. From its historical beginnings consultancy was dominated by large organisations and by an entrepreneurial orientation. Because of this established patterns of professionalisation have not been viable in the face of opposition from large firms seeking to define for themselves the nature of expertise and control access to it.

While consultants may be seen as trail blazers, similar tendencies can now be found in other, more established professions such as law, architecture and accountancy. In these sectors, too, there has been a strong tendency towards organisational consolidation with the larger firms becoming increasingly dominant. In the UK, for example, large law firms account for only 2 per cent of all law firms but employ over a third of all solicitors and generate 50 per cent of total professional revenues.[27] Such change has also gone hand in hand with a shift from occupational (or external) closure regimes, designed to regulate access to the profession, to organisational ones, concerned with managing training and progression within the internal labour markets of the firms themselves. The 'big four' global accounting firms, for example, have developed their own 'professional' development programmes, independently of professional associations and no longer rely on them for traditional support services.[28]

As we have seen, such tendencies also have implications for practitioners and clients. For employees in these organisations a shift towards more regulated or 'managed' work regimes may have unforeseen consequences for morale, future career aspirations and productivity. One possibility is that consulting work and the (increasingly) distant prospect of attaining elite partner status may lose its appeal. Indeed, it seems paradoxical that many large firms have gone down this route 'in the face of findings which suggest that, in order to promote organizational innovation and creativity, highly autonomous working conditions need to be provided'.[29]

The shift towards corporate professionalism also raises concern about regulation and the quality assurance of services. The IMC actively engages with its clients and involves them, through its Consultancy Purchasing Group, in the development of consultancy knowledge and practice. In 2002 the government also agreed best practice guidelines with the MCA on how to deliver better, more efficient consulting advice in the public sector. Such moves represent an attempt by consultants to regulate themselves, to establish some third party obligations and guarantee of quality above and beyond those of reputation and brand. But how far this kind of soft regulation will be effective in a context of weak professions and a Labour government in the UK, itself increasingly addicted to using management consultants,[30] remains to be seen.

Matthias Kipping is Professor of Strategic Management at York University; Ian Kirkpatrick is Professor of Work and Organisation at Leeds University; and Daniel Muzio is Lecturer in Organisation, Work and Technology at Lancaster University.

Notes

1   T Armbrüster and M Kipping, 'Strategy consulting at the crossroads: technical change and shifting market conditions for top-level advice', *International Studies of Management and Organisation* 32, no 4 (2003).

2   Kennedy Information, '30-year ranking database', *Consultants News*, Aug 2003.

3   For a full discussion see M Reed, 'Expert power and control in late modernity: an empirical review and theoretical synthesis', *Organization Studies* 17, no 4 (1996).

4   P Brown and A Hesketh, *The Mismanagement of Talent* (Oxford: Oxford University Press, 2004).

5   M Alvesson, 'Managing knowledge workers in the new economy', *UQ News Online*, 20 Feb 2006, see www.uq.edu.au/news/index.html?article=9023 (accessed 24 May 2006).

6   For a more detailed account of this history see M Kipping, 'Trapped in their wave: the evolution of management consultancies' in T Clark and R Fincham (eds), *Critical Consulting: New perspectives on the management advice industry* (Oxford: Blackwell, 2002).

7   I Kirkpatrick and M Kipping , 'The development of the management consultancy business: a co-evolution perspective', paper for the 4th International Critical Management Studies Conference, Cambridge, UK, 4–6 July 2005.

8   Kipping, 'Trapped in their wave'.

9   M Kipping and D Saint-Martin, 'Between regulation, promotion and consumption: government and management consultancy in Britain', *Business History* 47, no 3 (2005).

10 CD McKenna, 'The world's newest profession: management consulting in the twentieth century', *Enterprise and Society* 2 (2001).

11 M Alvesson, 'Social identity and the problem of loyalty in knowledge intensive companies', *Journal of Management Studies* 37, no 8 (2000).

12 T Morris and L Empson, 'Organization and expertise: an exploration of knowledge bases and the management of accounting and consulting firms', *Accounting, Organizations and Society* 23, no 5/6 (1998).

13 R Greenwood and L Empson, 'The professional partnership: relic or exemplary form of governance?', *Organization Studies* 24, no 6 (2003).

14 MT Hansen, N Nohria and T Tierney, 'What's your strategy for managing knowledge?', *Harvard Business Review* 77, no 2 (1999).

15 A Werr and T Stjernberg, 'Exploring management consulting firms as knowledge systems', *Organization Studies* 24, no 6 (2003).

16 M Kipping and C Amorim, 'Consultancies as management schools' in RP Amdam, R Kvalshaugan and E Larsen (eds), *Inside the Business Schools* (Oslo: Abstrakt, 2003).

17 See www.consulting-moneymachine.com/what.html (accessed 24 May 2006).

18 VW Mitchell, 'Problems and risks in the purchasing of consultancy services', *Service Industries Journal* 14, no 3 (1994).

19   T Clark, 'The market provision of management services, information
      asymmetries and service quality – some market solutions: an empirical
      example', *British Journal of Management* 4, no 4 (1993).
20   AV Bhide, 'Building the professional firm: McKinsey and Co.: 1939–1968', HBS
      Working Paper 95-010 (Boston: Harvard Business School, 1995, rev March
      1996).
21   *Wirtschaftswoche*, 2 Aug 1974.
22   'Joining the firm: training to be the best – the McKinsey Way', Part 2 of *Masters
      of the Universe*, TV series on management consultants for Channel 4, Films of
      Record (1999), see www.filmsofrecord.com (accessed 24 May 2006).
23   L Pinault, *Consulting Demons: Inside the unscrupulous world of global corporate
      consulting* (New York: Harper Business, 2000).
24   N Cohen, 'Natural born billers', *Observer*, 19 June 2005.
25   E Michaels, H Handfield-Jones and B Axelrod, *The War for Talent* (Boston, MA:
      Harvard Business School Press, 2001).
26   JA Byrne, 'Commentary: Investor power has its downside, too', *Business Week
      Online*, 1 July 2002, see
      www.businessweek.com/magazine/content/02_26/b3789026.htm (accessed 24
      May 2006).
27   D Muzio and S Ackroyd, 'On the consequences of defensive professionalism:
      the transformation of the legal labour process', *Journal of Law and Society* 32,
      no 4 (2005).
28   R Suddaby, D Cooper and R Greenwood, 'Trans national regulation of
      professional services: governance dynamics of field level organisational change',
      paper presented at 'Conceptualising professions' seminar, Said Business School,
      Oxford, 25 May 2004.
29   M Robertson and J Swan, 'Going public: the emergence and effects of soft
      bureaucracy within a knowledge intensive firm', *Organization* 11, no 1 (2004).
30   It is estimated that while in 1994 UK government expenditure on management
      consultants stood at £500 million, by 2004 this had risen to a staggering
      £1.9 billion. See Pinault, *Consulting Demons*.

Futures for professionalism

14. The profession of public service

Michael Bichard

I spent the first half of my career working in a local government sector which had literally been shaped by the professions. Departments were structured around planners, architects, accountants, social workers and surveyors. Their chief officers reported to their 'own' committees, reinforcing the power of the professional ethos. The equivalent of today's head of the paid service was usually a legally qualified town clerk who was quaintly regarded as 'primus inter pares'. He therefore struggled manfully (given the almost total lack of women in such positions) to develop some kind of corporacy in the authority. It was taken for granted that all this would be for the benefit of the public because, well, professionals had always worked for the good of their clients according to standards set by their professional peers. A specific customer focus was, therefore, unnecessary. Collaborations between the different professional departments tended to occur primarily in respect of a location (a retail redevelopment or housing regeneration) and was often fraught. Those of us who began to champion the use of corporate management participation and customer care were regarded by the professional majority as in a way betraying the profession.

When I moved to central government in 1990 I encountered a very different public service world almost devoid of professionals. Generalists were cherished, developed and promoted. The head of finance and personnel in the Department of Social Security with an expenditure budget of £100 billion and 85,000 staff had no professional training. No one thought that unusual. Interestingly there was the same lack of corporate behaviour as existed in local government and an even more cavalier approach to the customer, client, patient – victim or supplicant!

Of course both locally and centrally much has changed and in some ways those changes have produced some convergence. Interestingly the civil service is now in the throes of 'professionalising' policy formulation, delivery and specialist support. The service also has many more professionally qualified specialists. Local government, meanwhile, has gradually broken down the professional compartments, instead organising more around issues – children, for example. In doing so it has placed a stronger focus on the broader skills of management and leadership.

Child abuse cases such as Climbié have shown how professional boundaries can lead to poor communications between individuals serving a single client. The lack of shared cultures, training and even language have protected the status and identities of professional groups but at the expense of the clients' welfare. In a real sense professional boundaries can now be seen to have been designed for the convenience and protection of the professions not the client. As the emphasis shifts even more towards quality and client needs so the demand is for work to be redesigned in ways that make sense for the client and which, if possible, also achieve the more efficient use of resources. So we see not only children's services but the development of teaching assistants in the classroom and some signs of the line between nurses and doctors being blurred simply because it makes sense from the patient's point of view. In some extreme cases where professionals are in very short supply (eg occupational therapists) it has become necessary to redesign the job to ensure that clients receive the necessary support.

There has also been a shift in the balance of power between, on the one hand, the public service as a profession and, on the other, the traditional professions such as law, accountancy and surveying. As a young professional starting out in local government I was clear that the primary loyalty of most professional colleagues was to the profession not the service or even the authority. The subsequent debates about corporate and community planning and management, customer care, community engagement, diversity and the new public management have gradually developed a sense that public service management is in itself a profession so that many members of the traditional professions see themselves as having a kind of dual citizenship. They remain accountable to their professional bodies but they are more aware of a wider responsibility to their authority or department and to the community it serves. Consequently many are openly sympathetic to an agenda that emphasises the need for public services to be driven by the wishes of citizens and users not the producers.

Professionals in the public service have always plied their trade under pressure. They have been used to challenge from their political masters determined to fulfil manifesto commitments in the face of possibly unhelpful advice. And they have been expected to justify their advice to communities sometimes angry at its implications and their apparent inflexibility. In recent years the challenges from both sources have become much more intense. As politicians themselves have become more pressured – not least by the media – so they have exerted more pressure for the 'right' or the convenient professional advice. Equally, communities have become better organised and have access to information and knowledge never available before the advent of the internet. These same communities now even have the benefit of online campaign tools to make them ever more effective. As a result the life of the public service professional, never easy, is becoming more difficult. The respect close to reverence, which they could in the past take for granted, now has to be earned. And each reported example of professional error makes earning that respect more challenging. The best public service professionals never saw their task as solely transferring knowledge to politicians or communities but rather interpreting that knowledge for their benefit. Their continued credibility depends ever more on their ability to do that without damaging their apolitical status. The successful public professional needs therefore to develop an acute understanding of the particular political context in which they work if they are to operate effectively. Ministers want professional advice that has already been 'cooked' by exposure to the political realities of the time. Most do not welcome raw professional advice that they are expected to adapt to the real world.

The pressure experienced by professionals operating in these circumstances has never been fully understood by their own professional bodies. At times the employed lawyers, for example, have enjoyed a reduced status in their own profession. They have consequently been forced to rely on their own personal values and ethics in a way not perhaps experienced by colleagues operating in more traditional settings and that self-reliance may be serving them well in today's more exposed environment. They are not just self-reliant but perhaps even self-regulated.

The fact that professionals in the public service face so many shared experiences and pressures and the fact that there is now so much convergence between local government, central government and the health service makes it all the more surprising that the public service has remained so segmented. As the balance of emphasis shifts between the professional in the public service and the public service as a profession one question is whether there is now a case for establishing a single public service profession in the UK.

When the devolved administrations were established the then cabinet secretary was careful to ensure that a unified civil service was retained to ensure a continuing free flow of people and a commonality of values. But if these arguments are powerful *within* the civil service then they could be equally powerful and could be applied across the public sector. For a start a single public service profession would encourage much greater movement of staff to the benefit of everyone. It is currently difficult to persuade able young civil servants to go into local government or even health because they are fearful that the experience will not be valued or that they will be forgotten. It is even harder to arrange secondments from local to central government – although there are of course examples. As a result the level of understanding between the sectors is too low, to the detriment of policy-making and delivery. A wider pool of opportunities would make it easier for people to change career direction and find jobs more suited to their particular competencies. At the moment the different sectors are too suspicious of applicants who have not been 'grown' within that particular sector. There are too few examples of mobility.

The present artificial boundaries also discourage the free flow of ideas, experience, knowledge and good practice. Central government still has a tendency to 'look down' on local government and, as a result, has been reluctant to see the relevance of much of the good practice that has grown up there in recent years. Equally the health service remains for many a mysterious place – within which much good is taking place. Issues of leadership, management, service design and the creation of client service strategies are all common across the sectors and yet we now have separate local government leadership centres, a national school of government, a national leadership centre for schools and have even seen attempts to develop a 'national health university'. Perhaps a 'national school for public service leadership' is needed that could have a transformational effect on our public services, the quality of leadership and the definition and development of this public service profession.

A move towards some kind of public service profession could also help remove the artificial barriers which can exist even within single professional groups. When I joined the Department for Education and Employment there was, I think, only one person in the whole department who had had extensive experience of working in schools or in education authorities. It was Ray Shostak, who continued to break the mould by going back to local government to establish the Children's Services department in Hertfordshire and who is now back with central government at the Treasury. The problem was that there was no natural route from the classroom to the local education authority and thence to a senior position in government. That meant that front-line teachers did not see how they could move into central government to help shape directly the future of the education service.

They could contribute only when they were invited to do so and therefore felt disenfranchised with no sense of ownership of policy and every reason to criticise that policy. The same was true of health and housing and although action has been taken to improve the situation at the margins (more in some government departments than others) it is fundamentally unchanged. If an individual develops a passion for the profession in the front line surely it is right that they should have the opportunity to carry that passion and their knowledge to the minister's door if that is their wish and they develop the skills to achieve it?

And what stands in the way of this public service profession? Vested interests certainly. As ever the current system works in favour of those with the power. In addition many would be concerned that a single profession would change the balance of power and influence between officials or officers and the politicians. And of course the transitional problems, not least pay disparities, would be very significant. So maybe we should be defining a direction of travel rather than a single precisely defined destination. We should do more to encourage a sense that public service with client needs at its core is in itself a worthy professional calling. We should continue to change the balance of loyalty between the traditional professional groupings and the public service as a profession. We should minimise the barriers to mobility ensuring that the most important jobs are genuinely open to the very best people. And we should aspire to a public service that is structured to facilitate partnership working for the benefit of clients. A public service which ensures that good practice is more likely to be shared and bad practice more likely to be avoided. It is difficult to argue that we currently have public services organised in the way most likely to satisfy client needs so let's think radically about how they could be changed for the better.

Michael Bichard is Rector at the University of the Arts London.

15. Production by the masses

Professionals and postindustrial public services

Charles Leadbeater

Public service professionals seem stuck. Recruitment and retention to professions has become more difficult, as relative pay and status has declined; morale in many professions is low. Professionals in many public services complain they face more paperwork and bureaucracy, rules and regulations. They feel their jobs are being made more difficult and less rewarding as they drift further from the ideal of the independent skilled professional, making judgements, providing expertise, trusted by both clients and funders to do a good job. Yet public service clients do not seem to feel more in control, even though these constraints on professional discretion – the national curriculum, codes of best practice and risk management guides, inspection regimes – have been introduced in the name of serving people better. As a result many public service professionals feel at odds with the systems they work within.

We need a new account of what professionals do for society and the kinds of institutions in which they work, a set of new design principles to guide public service reform over the next two decades. Our aim should be to create postindustrial public services, which are more collaborative, networked and distributed. Public institutions and professionals should educate us towards self-help and self-reliance as much as possible. Modern society trains us to be workers and consumers. Postindustrial institutions should train us for self-management and self-assessment. That means restoring a proper balance between professional service and self-help. Resources, skills and tools have to be much more distributed, out of top-heavy, inflexible institutions and into communities and homes. We turn to professionals for their knowledge and judgement but we need far more than that. Postindustrial public services must promote motivation and cultural change. Motivation is the new medicine: motivating and equipping people to look after themselves better. Motivating children to want to continue exploring and learning should be one of the chief aims of the education system. That would mean the role of professionals in future would be to act as persuaders, counsellors and campaigners, not delivering a service, but encouraging people to acquire the skills to look after themselves more effectively.

Only a sustained programme of radical redesign, to shift public services and their professionals away from a perverted, semi-industrial format, in which they attempt to deliver solutions to waiting consumers, will deal with the deep sense of malaise that now afflicts most public service professions.

Social work is perhaps the prime example of this malaise. The goals of social work are enshrined in the International Federation of Social Work's definition, with its emphasis on prevention and unlocking personal potential. It says the mission of social work is to 'enable all people to develop their full potential, enrich their lives and prevent dysfunction'.[1] The Federation's definition goes on to describe the values of social work as based on 'respect for the inherent worth and dignity of all people', which entails respecting the right to self-determination; promoting the right to participation; treating each person as a whole within his or her family or community; and identifying and developing strengths, not just focusing on correcting for deficits or weaknesses. A leading academic study of social work concluded:

> *Good social work is doing with people and their families not to or for them. It requires a partnership between people and workers based on: mutual respect and trust; keeping the person*

*at the centre of the work; seeing the situation in the round;
enabling them to define desired outcomes and supporting them
to develop and own their own solutions.*[2]

Yet professionals, care staff and clients say the social work system
rarely delivers on these goals. It is not just the high-profile cases of
neglect and abuse. A sense of demoralisation seems to afflict the
entire profession. Professionals complain they can focus only on the
most difficult cases – such as children and families at risk – where
their role is to manage risk and police clients' behaviour rather than
help to change it. They do not have enough time to attend to the
complex issues and history that lie behind a client's need. They have
become gatekeepers to the system, managing access and entitlement
to help rather than engaging directly with clients. There is little or no
time for preventative or community-based work. As a result many
social workers feel they have no 'therapeutic' role and they are unable
to deliver on the values that drew them into the profession. The
mismatch between the avowed goals of the profession and the reality
of social work is a breeding ground for cynicism, disaffection and
demoralisation among professionals and clients alike.

Social work may be an extreme case. But that gap between the
public service professionals' avowed aims and the reality of their work
is gnawing away at all public service professions. Piecemeal reforms
seem to create as many problems as solutions. Workforce reform, the
creation of para-professionals, such as teaching assistants, to take
some of the burden off full professionals, provoke worries that
control is being diluted. Professionals could relinquish their role as
gatekeepers of resources, with all the angst and paperwork that goes
with that, but probably only by giving the consumers – patients,
parents, children, clients – more choice over how they want to spend
the resources allocated to them, perhaps in the form of direct
payments or individualised budgets. This makes many professionals
defensive. They argue that their clients often lack the knowledge and
skills to make intelligent choices. Professionals do not like being
managers, nor do they want to be managed. So in social work, for

example, the best professionals are often promoted into management, losing direct contact with their clients and working peers. Meanwhile, schemes designed in part to divert demand away from professionals, such as NHS Direct, seem to have made little difference to the sense of pressure.

Declining trust has also gnawed away at professional relationships with clients. Doctors and social workers have lost the ability they once enjoyed to speak without challenge about their patient's ills. Misdiagnosis, maltreatment, cover-ups of malpractice and political mobilisation by aggrieved patients combined mean that third-party regulators are now often inserted into the relationship between professional and client. But as a result feedback loops from dissatisfied users back to the professionals tend to be very extended; they go via inspectors and ombudsmen. Professionals feel less trusted, but users do not necessarily feel more empowered.

Many professionals have responded by reaching out to their clients in new ways. We turn to professionals primarily for their specialist knowledge, to provide us with diagnosis and explanation, to guide us to the best course of action if we want to learn maths, get our knee fixed or become a better parent.[3] Power is the ability not to have to explain what you are doing, or at least to do so in language so esoteric that it renders the listener dumb or makes them feel slow. Some people are attracted to professions because they have a vocation to serve, others because being a professional confers status and power. So it seems that many professionals – especially doctors perhaps – have been trained to give explanations in a way designed to keep the patient at bay. Yet consumer culture, combined with the spread of alternative sources of information and knowledge, now means that people do not want to be talked down to. They want to be treated as intelligent participants in a conversation, which takes place at a speed and in a language that allows them to contribute. People like metaphors and simple stories of cause and effect. Yet professionals often lapse into specialist codes, probabilities, risks and technicalities. Translating technical issues into accessible language is a skill that not all professionals have. Promotion and advancement within pro-

fessional communities comes from talking the language of the profession rather than that of the clients. Academics who are good at
communicating publicly, and so acquire a popular following, do not
always find that improves their professional standing.

All these supposed remedies – better communication, more
support staff, improved consumer information – attempt to reform
the professional's relationship with their clients, to make them fit for
a more demanding and less deferential age. All have some merit. But
there may be a deeper problem they fail to reach: the professional
service model itself may be ill suited to tackle many of the issues we
face as a society.

Health is a classic example of where employing many more professionals and paying them more does not guarantee results. Despite a
doubling of health spending since 1997, waiting times for routine
operations are set to climb in 2006/07 because of the funding crisis
within the NHS. Much of the additional spending has gone to employ
and pay for more nurses and doctors. The 2002 Wanless Review of the
future of the NHS, commissioned by the Treasury, suggested that on
current trends health spending would have to double again in the
next 20 years to keep pace with demand.[4] That is inconceivable. The
problem is rooted deep within the professional model of public
service delivery.

A modern health system, built around hospitals, is working
efficiently when the beds are full as much of the time as possible. The
aim must be to fill up the hospital. Yet a healthy society is one in
which people do not need to go to hospital nor to see doctors. The
best definition of health is not needing to see a doctor. The fact that
we associate good health care with hospitals that are full is a sign of
just how skewed our thinking has been by systems of industrial
production applied to social issues. The more that hospitals can
produce high-quality, personalised, mass, customised treatment,
along a more or less linear patient pathway that looks something like
a production line, the better health care we will get, we think. The
patient goes in at one end ill, is worked on by doctors and nurses, and
emerges out of the other, like a finished product, well again and, if

they are lucky, they get some after-sales service from social services.

The hospital-focused health care system emerged in response to the spread of contagious and acute disease born by urbanisation and industrialisation in the late nineteenth century. The aim was to provide a place where specially trained people – doctors and nurses – could repair people who were ill, a bit like a garage repairs a broken-down car. But now this system of professional diagnosis, prescription and monitoring has to face a challenge for which it was not designed: an epidemic of chronic disease, in a society in which people live for longer.

In the UK, 45 per cent of the adult population have one or more long-standing medical condition. Among those 75 years old, the fastest-growing group of the population, the figure is 75 per cent. By 2030 the proportion of 65-year-olds with a long-term condition will double. In 1900 circulatory diseases, like heart conditions and cancer, were responsible for 19 per cent of deaths: most people died too young to be troubled by a chronic condition. In 2004 circulatory diseases and cancer were responsible for 63 per cent of deaths. About 80 per cent of consultations with a general practitioner are about an aspect of a long-term condition. Another 10 per cent are for minor ailments and conditions that are best dealt with through self-treatment and over-the-counter drugs.

Chronic conditions are often linked together: people with five long-term conditions generally get more than 50 different prescriptions a year. About 650 million prescriptions a year go to people with long-term conditions. Chief among these conditions is diabetes. In the UK more than two million people are diagnosed diabetics and a further one million are diabetic without realising it. If type II diabetes, which is linked to lifestyle, is caught early its development can be kept in check. But a system in which expertise is inside clinics and hospitals does not allow us to diagnose diabetes early enough. Between 40 per cent and 50 per cent of diabetes is not diagnosed until it is too late. Then people become dependent on regular insulin injections, which in the UK involves repeat visits to the doctor and difficult changes to what they eat, how they cook and the rest of their lifestyle. The hospital-based health system, designed around professional expertise to treat contagious disease and cure people, is ill-designed to prevent and manage chronic long-term conditions.[5]

This mismatch between a professionalised hospital-focused health service and the needs of society will not be solved by employing more para-professional nurses, tighter regulation of medical ethics or doctors talking in the vernacular to patients, though all have their place. We need a much more radical rethinking of the role of professions, their relations with their clients and the organisations that bring them together. We have created systems for the mass production of public goods through schools, hospitals and social work departments run by professionals. In future more of the emphasis will have to be production by the masses not for them. Which is where Ivan Illich comes in.

Ivan Illich was a nomadic and iconoclastic Catholic priest and arch critic of industrial society in the 1970s who in a series of polemical and passionate books – more like pamphlets – set about the failings of modern institutions and the professionals who organise them: *Deschooling Society, Limits to Medicine, Disabling Professions* and *Tools for Conviviality*.[6]

As he put it in *Deschooling Society*:

> The pupil is 'schooled' to confuse teaching with learning, grade advancement with education, a diploma with competence, and fluency with the ability to say something new. His imagination is 'schooled' to accept service in place of value. Medical treatment is mistaken for health care, social work for the improvement of community life, police protection for safety, military poise for national security, the rat race for productive work. Health, learning, dignity, independence and creative endeavour are defined as little more than the performance of the institutions which claim to serve these ends, and their improvement is made to depend on allocating more resources to

the management of hospitals, schools and other agencies in question.[7]

Illich was ahead of his time by being behind the times: his critique of industrialisation harked back to pre-industrial, communal forms of organisation, as well as foreseeing a world of networks and webs long before the internet. For much of the 1970s he was a darling of the left, sharing some intellectual common ground with Herbert Marcuse and the Frankfurt School's critique of a one-dimensional society, run by large corporations. He was an environmentalist before the movement had been born and lived a spartan life with few possessions. Yet Illich was no lefty. Although he was deeply at odds with the Vatican, he never left the Catholic priesthood. He dismayed many of his left-wing fans with a withering attack on Castro's Cuba and his defence of the traditional gender roles, which enraged feminists. Illich was both radical, profoundly conservative and yet also a libertarian, an early advocate of a version of education vouchers and individual choice in public services. Illich died in 2002 and towards the end of his life his writing became more apocalyptic, at times melancholy and pessimistic.

Yet in a short, golden period in the mid-1970s, Illich set out not just a critique of industrial-era institutions and their professionals but also some highly suggestive ideas on how they might find a more supportive, realistic and balanced role in society. Those ideas now have even more relevance.

After Ivan Illich trained as a priest he went to work in a poor Puerto Rican neighbourhood in New York City and he was struck by how many other institutions seemed to be modelled on the church and how many professions seemed to take their cue from the priesthood. Illich's argument against the church was that it turned the charity and mutuality evident in the tale of the Good Samaritan into a kind of social machine. The church became not just a source of care and solace, but a source of power and doctrine, in which the priesthood determined who was holy. For Illich this perversion of care into the exercise of power was the fate of all institutions and caring professions. Mutual support and care mutated into the institutionalised welfare state with its rules and entitlements. Curiosity and a desire to learn, for the sake of living a more fulfilled life, became an education system that grades people by how well they learn what the system decides.

The triumph of modern industrial society, according to Illich, is the creation of institutions on a vast scale, which provide services such as education, health and policing that might have once been limited to just a few. These universal systems aspire to deliver services that are fair and reliable. Yet that in turn requires codes, protocols and procedures, which often make them dehumanising. These institutions and the resources they control become the power base for the new priesthoods: the public service professionals.

The original, liberal professions were independent, small-scale and localised. They worked in a society where knowledge was scarce and difficult to access and so people had no option but to cope themselves. The liberal professions become dominant professions, according to Illich, with the institutionalisation of their knowledge and power into systems. Dominant professions do not just provide services and solutions, they also define what we need and what we lack. Not only are the professions a powerful vested interest in society, attracting resources and prestige, they also dominate the way we think. Even though most improvements in health have come from changes in lifestyle, the way we work, public health and food, in the public imagination health is indelibly associated with doctors and hospitals, men and women in white coats.

The dominance of professions creates two big problems according to Illich: counterproductivity and a dependency culture.

Professional institutions become counterproductive: the more resources that are poured into them, the more problems and ill effects they create, often outweighing the benefits. A hospital that provides a cure for a specific medical condition – an elderly person's broken hip – can quickly disorient the patient and rob them of self-confidence, as they are passed from doctor to doctor, ward to ward. It takes only a few days for an elderly person in hospital to lose their self-confidence in their own capacity to cope. They are likely to emerge with their hip cured but their self-confidence shattered. The apparent omnipotence of doctors, the mystique of the profession, excites people to expect cures that cannot be delivered. When the doctor cannot dispense the expected cure, it breeds a sense of frustration and disappointment that leads to a loss of trust.[8]

This counterproductivity also afflicts education, he argues. The school system is meant to be a route for social mobility and opportunity. Yet any system of ranking and grading is bound to produce failures and dropouts as much as successes. Indeed far from encouraging people to learn, formal schooling trains people to turn off. School creates the impression that learning is the product of teaching and something we do only in special places, like schools, at special times in our lives, with the help of special people: accredited teachers. Education is seen as unworldly; to learn is to be cut off from the day-to-day world. But by extension the world – where we live most of our lives – cannot be about learning. Education is seen not as a personal project but as a process of certification to show you have learned what the system expects.

As people become more dependent on professionals so they lose faith in their own capacity to act. The rise of professional power is mirrored by a loss of individual responsibility. We become cases to be processed by the system rather than participants. Education and health come to be commodities to be acquired rather than capabilities we develop in ourselves to live better lives.

For Illich, professionalised institutions are nightmares forged out of good intentions. The professions that serve us disable us at the same time. As Charles Taylor, the philosopher, puts it in the introduction to *The Rivers North of the Future*, a collection of Illich's last writings:

> *Ours is a civilisation conceived to relieve suffering and enhance human well-being on a universal scale, unprecedented in human history. It's what we think we ought to be able to do and yet we also feel that those very systems can imprison us in forms that turn alien and dehumanising.*[9]

Many public service professionals may feel confused, aggrieved and astounded by Illich's critique, which is easy to dismiss as utopian and naïve. However, because he was prepared to think fundamentally his analysis also yields suggestive ideas about how professionals might repair their relations with the people they serve.

As he put it in his most optimistic book, *Tools for Conviviality*:

> *I believe a desirable future depends on our deliberately choosing a life of action over a life of consumption, on our engendering a lifestyle which will enable us to be spontaneous, independent, yet related to each other, rather than maintaining a lifestyle which only allows us to produce and consume.*[10]

Postindustrial, convivial institutions would work through conversation rather than instruction; co-creation between users and producers, learners and teachers, rather than delivery; mutual support among peers as much as professional service.

In *Deschooling Society*, first published in the UK in 1971, he provided some principles for how a more convivial education system would work, for example, by providing all who want to learn with access to resources at any time, in airports, factories, offices, museums and libraries as well as schools; making it easy for those who want to share knowledge to connect with those who want to learn from them through skills exchanges and directories of classes that people could choose from; allowing those who want to propose an issue for discussion and learning to do so easily. In 1971 that sounded radical and far-fetched. In the era of Wikipedia and eBay, blogs and Slashdot, Monster.com and MeetUp it sounds more like the conventional wisdom of the social networks created by the internet. Illich's argument was that education should be a delicate blend of the personal and the collective: learning should be driven by what a person feels motivated and curious about and they should be able to draw easily from common resources to achieve their ends.

Illich's proposals in *Tools for Conviviality*, *Deschooling Society* and *Limits to Medicine* yield the following six design principles for public services and professionals in a postindustrial society.

First, public institutions and professionals should educate us towards self-help and self-reliance as much as possible. Modern society trains us to be workers and consumers. Postindustrial institutions should train us for self-management and self-assessment. As Illich put it in *Deschooling Society*: 'Good institutions encourage self-assembly, re-use and repair. They do not just serve people but create capabilities in people, support initiative rather than supplant it.' In *Limits to Medicine*, he argued: 'Better health care will depend not on some new therapeutic standard but on a level of willingness and competence to engage in self-care.' Almost 30 years later the Wanless Review of health spending reached exactly the same conclusion. We will become a healthy society only if we restore the proper balance between professional service and self-help. Illich's golden rule was that formal instruction must never outweigh opportunities for independent learning.

Second, this means public services need to build our capacity for self-assessment and self-evaluation, starting with education. The modern, professional state spends massive sums on assessing need, especially in social care, where perhaps a third of the budget goes on assessment of need by professionals. First professionals assess what we need, whether we are entitled to state support and then they determine how that should be delivered. Then more professionals, in the form of inspectors, come along to check it has all been done properly. We need much greater emphasis on intelligent self-assessment and self-evaluation. That is already the lynchpin of the tax system and should play a greater role in education and health. Experiments with self-assessment in social care show that people generally do not over-claim benefits and are more likely to see how they could address their needs without turning to the state. The education system schools us to think of assessments as exams, something we do at the end of the pipeline, checked by a professional. We need an education system that builds up capacity for intelligent self-evaluation, so that we are better equipped to assess and solve problems under our own steam, with the help of our peers and professionals if needed.

Third, as well as imparting knowledge, postindustrial public services must promote motivation and cultural change. Motivation is the new medicine: motivating and equipping people to look after themselves better. Motivating children to want to continue exploring and learning should be one of the chief aims of the education system. Schools instil a deference to professionals from an early age.

Whenever someone comes into contact with a public service it should not just deliver something to them, but also try to create the motivation for the person to look after themselves more effectively. For Illich this meant turning away from a consumerist account of public services in which we are served by others or acquire an education. Instead of having, acquiring, possessing, we should want a society that encourages action, doing, being. As he put it in *Limits to Medicine*:

> *In an intensely industrialised society, people are conditioned to get things rather than to do them; they are trained to value what can be purchased rather than what they themselves can create. They want to be taught, moved, treated or guided, rather than to learn, to heal and to find their own way.*[11]

That would mean the role of professionals in future would be to act as persuaders, counsellors and campaigners, not delivering a service, but encouraging people to acquire the skills to look after themselves more effectively. Such professionals would almost have be like molecules in the bloodstream of society, rather than waiting in their institutionalised boxes for the public to present their problems.

In *Limits to Medicine*, Illich described the goal of making health a personal task, which people take responsibility for, this way:

> *Success in this personal task is in large part the result of the self-awareness, self-discipline, and inner resources by which each person regulates his own daily rhythm and actions, his diet and sexual activity. . . . The level of public health corresponds to the degree to which the means and responsibility for coping with illness are distributed among the total population.*[12]

The implication is that the chief goal of professionals should be to serve people in a way that helps to build up this distributed capacity for coping. Service users need instead to see themselves as contributors, participants, investors in and taking responsibility for their own wellbeing.

Fourth, we will learn as much from our peers as from professionals. Postindustrial public services will not just provide professionals to be consulted but mobilise knowledge and expertise from a wide variety of sources. Professionals will still be the most knowledgeable and the best-resourced players in any field. But they will increasingly find themselves playing alongside alternative practitioners, para-professionals, peers and pro-ams.[13] Enlightened professionals will realise their jobs are made a lot easier if they relinquish their claim to a monopoly on knowledge and encourage people to turn to other, reliable sources. Thanks to the internet and new generations of search engines, people will increasingly find their way to the sources of news and information they trust. Professional monopolies on knowledge, painstakingly established in the twentieth century, will erode rapidly in the twenty-first century. Professionals will still provide expertise and judgement but they will also encourage exchange and encounter between peers.

Fifth, resources, skills and tools have to be much more distributed. *Tools for Conviviality* is a defence of simple, easy to use, vernacular tools that help people achieve things more easily, as opposed to complex tools that only professionals can understand and operate. Illich mainly wrote before the advent of the personal computer, the internet and the mobile phone. In later life he was no great fan of them. Yet in many ways these are great examples of the convivial, easy to access tools that allow people to collaborate and communicate. We have only just begun to tap their potential. Kent County Council is just starting trials of new home-based sensors to allow remote monitoring of the movements and health of elderly people, which should allow more to live in their own homes rather than move into care homes. In Korea a mobile phone came onto the market in 2006 that allows a person with diabetes to check their blood sugar levels and communicate the results to a doctor. Or take a thrombosis prevention service run in north London, which has 5,000 patients taking drugs to reduce blood pressure and risk of clotting. They have weekly blood tests, which are administered locally by nurses and GPs and sent in centrally for assessment. The unit writes to anyone who needs to change their dosage; if it is urgent they call them on the phone. The system works efficiently: tests are done by 11am and the results are back by 1.30pm. But in Germany the patients do all this themselves with a small machine that costs about £400. They do the test whenever they like. They analyse the results and change their dosage accordingly. In north London only ten of the 5,000 patients use this machine. The unit employs scores of nurses to do tests at industrial scale which could easily be done by the patients themselves.

Finally, it is not just tools that need to be distributed but finance as well. In the autumn of 2005 I spent an afternoon with a group of inspiring parents in Wigan who were all participating in the Department of Health's 'In Control' pilots to allow families caring for young people with learning disabilities to have individualised budgets. The group said that when they had been consumers of public services, they tended to complain to get things changed; they were often at odds with service providers and rarely shared ideas and resources among themselves. Once they became budget holders they started to look for ways to make the money go further; they worked more collaboratively with their care workers and with one another. Individualised budgets turned them from passive and often disempowered consumers into participants and players; they took responsibility for how their budget was spent.

Even now, three decades after Illich first sketched these design principles, they can sound utopian. It is certainly far-fetched to hope that public services could be reformed, in a single bound, to adopt this highly distributed approach. Public services and their professionals have developed through a process of sedimentation.

Schools, hospitals and welfare institutions started through acts of charity or faith. Professionals began life as independent advisers. They were brought together in the twentieth century into systems that could deliver public services at national scale, for everyone, at reasonable costs and standards through an uneasy truce between professional discretion and industrial process. Since the 1980s that has been overlaid by the growing weight of the 'McKinsey state' of performance management, targets, contracting out and quality standards. Current initiatives to extend choice will provide a thin topsoil of consumerism to systems that are still largely planned, rationed and dominated by professionals. Public spending programmes, by default or design, entrench and embed this industrialised model of service delivery. Despite a doubling of spending since 1997 the current crisis in hospital funding is squeezing out resources for preventative and social care. In education a massive capital programme is 'Building Schools for the Future', many of which will look alarmingly like schools of the recent past, with jazzier architecture. We incarcerate more people than ever, in prisons that look very like Strangeways, opened more than a century ago.

At the edges of these vast, asset-heavy, inflexible systems we can see the first signs of what postindustrial public services might look like: Kent's home-based social care programme; the 'In Control' initiative to give services users individualised budgets; the development of distance and peer-to-peer learning; and the 2006 social care white paper, which foresees the creation of a stronger infrastructure of community-based services. More important still, many of the most dynamic emerging business models are highly collaborative, peer-to-peer and distributed, from eBay and Craigslist to Linux open source software and computer games such as the Sims.

Postindustrial public services offer more than a new layer of sediment. They would reconfigure the geology of public services. That will not happen in a single comprehensive spending review, nor even a single parliament. But over 20 years it should be possible, indeed it will become a necessity, because our inherited, inflexible and often impersonal models of service will not be able to cope with projected levels of demand. Public services for the coming century, in the developing world even more than in the developed, should be distributed, collaborative, peer-to-peer, co-created and motivational.

Professionals will play a critical role in them dispensing advice, supporting clients, campaigning for cultural change, navigating access to resources and promoting self-help. They should become campaigners, counsellors and advocates rather than priests. Ivan Illich's genius was that 30 years ago he could already see this would not just be desirable but it would become a necessity.

Charles Leadbeater is a Demos associate.

Notes

1   International Federation of Social Work, see www.ifsw.org (accessed 26 May 2006).
2   C Leadbeater and H Lownsbrough, *Personalisation and Participation: The future of social care in Scotland* (London: Demos, forthcoming).
3   C Tilly, *Why?* (Princeton, NJ: Princeton University Press, 2006).
4   D Wanless, *Securing Our Future Health: Taking a long-term view*, final report (London: HM Treasury, April 2002).
5   H Cottam and C Leadbeater, *Health: Co-creating services*, Red paper 01 (London: Design Council, 2004).
6   Illich's books have been reprinted many times and are published in the UK by Marion Boyars Publishers, www.marionboyars.co.uk (accessed 21 May 2006), and distributed by Central Books.
7   I Illich, *Deschooling Society* (London: Marion Boyars Publishers, 1970, reissued 2002).
8   I Illich, *Limits to Medicine* (London: Marion Boyars Publishers, 1995), first published as *Medical Nemesis: The expropriation of health*, originally published in January 1975.
9   *The Rivers North of the Future: The testament of Ivan Illich*, as told to D Cayley, foreword by C Taylor (Toronto: House of Anansi Press, 2005).
10 I Illich, *Tools for Conviviality* (New York: Harper Row, 1973).
11 I Illich, *Limits to Medicine*.
12 Ibid.
13 C Leadbeater and P Miller, *The Pro-Am Revolution: How enthusiasts are changing our economy and society* (London: Demos, 2004).

16. Gender and professionalism

Hilary De Lyon

It is almost a century since the Sex Disqualification (Removal) Act 1919 allowed women for the first time to become members of professional associations. By 2003/04 women formed at least half of the entrants to many of the traditionally male-dominated professions including law (60 per cent), medicine (60 per cent), dentistry (60 per cent) and accountancy (50 per cent).[1] By contrast, shortly afterwards, on the 30th anniversary of the Sex Discrimination Act 1976, the Equal Opportunities Commission (EOC) published a report on women's representation.[2] It showed that, while women had made 'great strides', they still make up 'just 9 per cent of the judiciary, 10 per cent of senior police officers and 13 per cent of national newspaper editors'. With the numbers of women increasing substantially in many of the traditionally male professions in the UK, why does the leadership of the professions continue to be dominated by men, and have women had any impact on the culture of the professions?

While 30 years ago we might have expected weight of numbers alone to achieve radical change, today it is clear that our notions of professionalism and career advancement are more deeply affected by gender. By exploring some of the inroads women have made into traditionally male-dominated professions in recent decades and the changing context in which these efforts continue, we can begin to explore where more fundamental change might come from.

The question of numbers

Simply increasing the number of women in a profession has not been sufficient to create cultural change. For example, by 2004, 42 per cent of solicitors were women,[3] compared with 5 per cent in the late 1970s.[4] This change coincided with a dramatic increase in the size of this branch of the legal profession, which has more than doubled in size since 1980.[5] Despite the potential that this rise in numbers created for the profession to change and for women to reach senior positions, women have not made a significant impact at the top of the profession and only 22 per cent of partners in solicitors' firms in the UK are women.[6] Women tend to predominate in areas such as employment and family law and they are more likely to be employed in public sector legal posts than in private practice.[7] The numbers are lowest in the specialisms connected with commerce, which tend to be the highest earning and the most influential within the profession.

Women priests in the established church provide a particularly interesting example in looking at women's impact on traditionally male professions, since they have been excluded from priesthood by law until very recently. The first deacons (permitted to fulfil all the roles of a priest except presiding at communion and absolving sins or giving blessings) were ordained in 1987, but women were not permitted to enter the full priesthood until 1994. Yet although it has been only 12 years since women were first ordained, they already make up over 20 per cent of clergy (excluding bishops) and 50 per cent of those entering training. However, while women now hold 50 per cent of the non-stipendiary (ie unpaid) posts held by priests, they hold only one in six of the stipendiary (ie paid) posts and one in five of the chaplaincy (also paid) posts. A few women have been promoted to senior positions including two deans (the highest position below that of bishop). Women are still prevented by law from filling the highest leadership roles in the Church of England, and the issue of women bishops is currently under discussion within the synod, the presiding body of the church, though it appears likely that the necessary legislative changes will be made in the near future.

However, the picture in professions where women are the majority is hardly more encouraging. In medicine the proportion of women medical graduates approached 50 per cent in 1991 and is now 70 per cent, but only 25 per cent of consultants in hospital practice and 7 per cent of consultant surgeons are women.[8] Even in professions where women traditionally dominate numerically, such as nursing and teaching, the senior positions are disproportionately held by men. Only 10 per cent of nurses in the UK are male[9] and on average their qualifications are poorer[10] yet 'men are more likely to be promoted than women'.[11] Likewise while only 45.3 per cent of secondary school teachers are men, 65 per cent of headteachers are men.[12]

Barriers to professional leadership

Why then have the increasing levels of women's participation within traditionally male professions not led to a greater number of women in senior roles and a greater impact on those professions? Recent research suggests that the most important barriers to women's advancement include the challenge of combining work at senior levels and family life, stereotyping and inhospitable organisational culture, lack of role models and exclusion from formal networks.[13]

Flexible working

At present, the fact that most women have children at some time during the first 20 years after they qualify in their profession means not only that the pattern of their career is different from men, but the focus of their life also tends to be different in that they often find themselves in the position of having to balance formal paid employment with unpaid domestic and caring work. For this reason they are more likely to want to work flexibly.

Women doctors are more likely to choose general practice than other medical specialisms,[14] making up 60 per cent of GP registrars in England.[15] Research from the 1980s suggests that this is in order to secure early financial security and flexible work, which gives women better opportunities to combine professional and domestic responsibilities. As further evidence of the flexibility associated with the choice of general practice, one study showed that, among doctors, proportionately more women GPs worked part-time (51.2%) than hospital doctors (41.9%).[16] However, even in general practice, flexible work is under threat, with the recent cuts to the funding and management of the Flexible Careers Scheme for GPs in England, which run counter to government's recognition of the importance of flexible working for women in managing their careers.[17] And though one in three GPs in 1998 was a woman, they made up only a quarter of GP principals.[18]

As this suggests, it appears that in some fields part-time and flexible working may not be seen as compatible with being a professional. In medicine, for example, where continuity of care is highly valued, working full-time may be regarded as an essential feature of professionalism: 'The essence of professionalism has always been that its members work full-time: knowledge is too extensive for a part-time commitment.'[19] While there has been an increase in flexible working by men in general practice, they tend to do so later in their career as a prelude to retirement, when it cannot harm their promotion prospects.[20]

Competition and the service culture in the private sector can make flexible work difficult to achieve. For example, solicitors with international clients cannot simply leave the office at the end of the day and forget work until the following morning. They are expected to be accessible all the time. But there is a danger that the real demands of the profession will be masked by a culture of 'presenteeism' where it is not necessary to be doing anything, but simply to be seen to be present. According to Carole Howlett, chief of staff to the Commissioner of the Metropolitan Police, this is common in the police force.[21] While the police, like other organisations, have good policies for part-time and flexible working, many middle managers see them as a problem to manage rather than a means to keep good officers in post.

Flexible working for both sexes throughout their careers would enable men as well as women to take responsibility not only for child rearing, but also for running the home. This would have a beneficial effect for both sexes and would open up opportunities for men as well as women.

Stereotyping and preconceptions

Sometimes the reasons why women are unable to make progress within a profession arise from a failure to recognise the benefits of the skills particularly associated with women. For example, one of the main reasons still used as to why women cannot go into construction professions (including architecture, surveying and civil engineering) is the building site. While the reasons given focus on the physical characteristics of the site, Greed found that the real problems were social.[22] Much of the work on building sites involves managing people, which might well be attractive to women. Women were therefore being excluded from the area of the profession where interpersonal management skills were much needed.

Culture

Perhaps the most difficult barrier to overcome, because most deep-rooted, is that of culture. The very concept of professions and professionalism is one created and developed by men:

> Work that traces women's struggles to enter the professions in the late nineteenth and early twentieth century has suggested that these were not just a matter of doors and minds being closed to women, but of values that were embedded in the notion of the practice of a profession reflecting a masculine project and repressing or denying those qualities culturally assigned to femininity.[23]

While generations of women have entered male professions, therefore, they have not always found professional culture hospitable. For example, Fondas distinguishes between cultures often associated with females – which emphasise caring relationships and egalitarian systems – and those associated with males – which emphasise impersonal relationships and hierarchical systems. She suggests that women value affiliation, attachments and relationships as highly or more highly than self-enhancement.[24] However, for solicitors in private practice, for instance, the shift has in fact been towards individualism. The introduction of competition in the 1980s changed the character of the profession from one of gentlemanliness to one of entrepreneurship, which has tended to exacerbate the barriers already experienced by women in achieving equality and making an impact on the field.

A report by the Federation of the Royal Colleges of Physicians noted that in medicine male-dominated specialities such as surgery, anaesthetics, and obstetrics and gynaecology are in fact popular career choices for women, but fewer progress beyond senior house officer grade than would be expected.[25] In surgery recent research shows that the perception of male domination is one of the main reasons why women do not consider surgery as a career.[26]

More than a numbers game

Ensuring that women participate in a profession in large numbers may be necessary to achieve change but is far from sufficient. Why is this? Helen Thorne argues that the first women priests in the Church of England held a collaborative leadership style, with a majority of respondents revealing a strong identification with cooperative ways of working. She suggested that the reason for this collaborative approach was that women had initially adopted collaborative working patterns in order to survive patriarchal structures in society and that they had found that this alternative approach became a source of strength and empowerment for them. Thorne concluded that women bring a different, fresh approach to the ordained ministry, but:

> It was clear that women priests are far from united in their understanding of the need for change in the Church, nor did they necessarily enter the Church with a specific agenda for transformation. These factors, coupled with an ambivalence towards feminism, seriously limit women's capacity to be radical agents for the Church's transformation.[27]

In contrast, among female politicians, almost three-quarters of the 100 new Labour women MPs elected in 1997 identified themselves as feminists.[28] Though their definitions of feminism varied widely, the unifying themes reflected beliefs in women's autonomy and equality. Childs's interviews showed that the majority of new Labour women MPs considered that they had articulated women's concerns in the House, that women constituents had accessed them in greater numbers and that they had developed contacts with women's organisations in their constituency. As far as style of politics was concerned, many of the women MPs considered that there was a feminised style, but that it was less well regarded than the 'ya-boo' dominant masculine style. There was some recognition that the 'women MPs' ability to transform the parliamentary political agenda is likely to be reduced if they act like women; acting for women might be dependent upon acting like men'.

It is possible to identify ways in which the House of Commons has changed since 1997. In particular the hours during which the House sits have been changed substantially, so that they are more family friendly, though there has not been universal support for this initiative. Barbara Follett MP, chair of the Women's Parliamentary Labour Party, sees change in Parliament as very much work in progress and thinks that women 'will probably not get anywhere until we reach a critical mass (around 25–30%) on both sides of the House and can push through changes in the whips' offices. It is they who keep the archaic and arcane practices and inhuman hours going. They use it as a means of disciplining their troops.'[29]

As this contrast suggests, changing professions is far more than just a numbers game – it requires real dynamism and determination and the ability to win a broad base of support.

Building a sustainable, fair professionalism

Despite the statistics on participation, much work remains to be done in opening up the upper echelons of our professions. As we look to the future of this work, there are reasons for both optimism and concern. While demographic and social change continue to push professions to achieve full equality, there are equally strong pressures resisting change.

Perhaps most importantly, our ageing population means that some professions may face imminent shortages of leadership. To retain and develop all kinds of leadership, new and diverse forms of leadership and leadership development will have to be found. For example, work looking at the succession of headteachers and medical consultants is evidence that public pressure is already being felt in this area. Stereotyping and poor work–life balance will have to be addressed urgently, not only to achieve justice but to enable public service reform.

However, the EOC argues that the pace of change is too slow and argues that the private sector should be given the same proactive duty as is being imposed on the public sector to promote equality and eliminate sex discrimination. But change will be truly effective only if attitudes evolve alongside legal and structural change, and this is unlikely to happen quickly. So while there is reason for optimism, there is certainly no room for complacency in the foreseeable future.

There is also a worrying dynamic that suggests professional culture change is too often won at the price of professional status. For example, in the house-building sector of the construction professions nearly half the membership of the Institute of Housing are women. While according to many women the work is similar to that of construction, one study reported that several of the male professionals distinguished between housing and construction, regarding the former as not 'real' building.[30] In other words: 'Once a specialism is seen as being suitable for women it seems to lose much of its power and status and *post hoc* reasons, structures and rules are created to legitimate the situation.' Similarly, this was a concern raised by Professor Carol Black, President of the Royal College of Physicians, about medicine.[31] And in relation to the priesthood, one of the leaders among the opponents to women priests in the Church of England, The Revd Geoffrey Kirk of Forward in Faith, was quoted as saying: 'Very soon the priesthood will be seen as a "hobby for grannies".[32] We need to ensure that professional reform makes public interest and not prejudice the basis for professional status.

In making the most of these opportunities and dealing with these threats, professionals themselves must make a concerted effort. First, women professionals still have an important role in leading professional culture change and providing positive role models. The contrast between progress in the church and in parliament shows the potential of concerted professional demands. While huge progress has been made in terms of participation, professional women can justifiably press employers and regulators to help open up professional leadership. Men also have a responsibility to enable change, which will ultimately benefit both sexes by opening up opportunities and improving the balance between work and home life.

Second, all professionals, together with professional associations, can make a real contribution by understanding the reasons why women do not reach the top and by seeking to accelerate changes in attitude. For example, the Royal Institute of British Architects sponsored a study into the reasons why a disproportionate number of women leave architecture,[33] and has developed an action programme to respond to its findings. Within surgery, the perception of male domination is one of the main reasons why women do not consider surgery as a career.[34] To counter this, in 1991 the Royal College of Surgeons of England set up Women in Surgical Training (WIST), to promote surgery as a career for women and to support women who have chosen surgery as a career. Initiatives include a national network of women in surgery and schools workshops for 16–17-year-old girls with talks and practical activities led by female consultant surgeons. Similarly, the Association of Women Solicitors (AWS) aims to provide support for women through a variety of mechanisms such as encouraging flexible working, a mentoring scheme, and a returner course for those taking a career break, which is also open to men.

So what can we conclude from all this? Clearly we have come a long way since Elizabeth Garrett Anderson fought her way into the medical profession in the mid-nineteenth century.[35] But we still have a long way to go. The first woman to reach the top of the legal profession by becoming a Law Lord, Baroness Hale, advises in relation to the legal profession that: 'Young women should not delude themselves that just because some things have changed, the struggle for equality is all over.'[36] This is absolutely true, but we also need to recognise that the aspirations of women may well be different from those of men, and that for women, reaching the top may not necessarily be the sole or even the most important criterion for judging professional success. We also need to accept that we all have a responsibility for achieving gender equality, and that this is not a problem for women alone to solve. Society as a whole will benefit from opening up opportunities for women to access positions of leadership in the professions. The question we each need to ask ourselves is how can we contribute to achieving this much needed change.

Hilary De Lyon is Chief Executive Officer of the Royal College of General Practitioners.

With thanks to Alyssa Joye, Demos intern, for help with the research for this essay.

Notes

1   A Langlands, *The Gateways to the Professions Report* (Nottingham: DfES Publications, July 2005).
2   Equal Opportunities Commission, *Sex and Power: Who runs Britain? 2006* (Manchester: EOC, 2006).
3   Law Society, *Annual Statistical Report* (2005), see: www.lawsociety.org.uk/ aboutlawsociety/whatwedo/researchandtrends/statisticalreport.law (accessed 2 June 2006).
4   Law Society Strategic Research Unit, *Trends in the Solicitors' Profession: Annual statistical report* (London: Law Society, 2004).
5   The Law Society, *Number of Solicitors on the Roll and Practising Certificate Holders since 1950* (London: Law Society, 2005).
6   S Bolton and D Muzio, 'The paradoxical processes of feminisation in the professions: the case of established, aspiring and semi-professions', Lancaster University Management School Working Paper 2005/048, 2005.
7   Law Society, *Annual Statistical Report.*
8   Association of Women Solicitors, *LINK* 15 (Autumn 2004).
9   Langlands, *Gateways to the Professions.*

10 'Male nurses overtake female nurses on career ladder', *BBC News online*, 5 Aug 1998, see http://news.bbc.co.uk/1/hi/health/146098.stm (accessed 21 May 2006).

11 LR Finlayson and JY Nazroo, *Gender Inequalities in Nursing Careers* (London: Policy Studies Institute, 1998).

12 M Coleman, *Gender and Headship in the 21st Century* (Nottingham, National College for School Leadership, 2004), see www.ncsl.org.uk/media/B13/B7/twlf-gender-and-headship.pdf (accessed 20 May 2006).

13 Opportunity Now, *Breaking the Barriers: Women in senior management in the UK* (London: Catalyst and Opportunity Now, 2000).

14 M Baker, 'The medical workforce in primary care: an investigation of the utilisation of vocationally trained doctors', Doctor of Medicine thesis (Nottingham: University of Nottingham, Sept 2001).

15 Royal College of General Practitioners, 'Profile of general practitioners, information sheet no 1', London: RCGP, 2005.

16 Davidson, quoted in Baker, 'The medical workforce in primary care'.

17 Women and Work Commission, *Shaping a Fairer Future*, Women and Equality Unit report (London: DTI Publications, 2006).

18 Royal College of Physicians, *Women in Hospital Medicine: Career choices and opportunities*, report of a working party of the Federation of Royal Colleges of Physicians (London: RCP, June 2001).

19 Baker, quoted in A Abbott, *The System of Professions: An essay on the divisions of expert labour* (Chicago: University Chicago Press, 1988).

20 Leese and Young 1999, quoted in Baker, 'The medical workforce in primary care'.

21 Association of Women Solicitors.

22 C Greed, 'Women in the construction professions: achieving critical mass', *Gender, Work and Organization* 7, no 3 (2000).

23 C Davies, 'The sociology of the professions and the profession of gender', *Sociology* 30, no 4 (1996).

24 N Fondas, 'Feminization unveiled: management qualities in contemporary writings', *Academy of Management Review* 22, no 1 (1997).

25 Federation of Royal College of Physicians, *Women in Hospital Medicine: Career choices and opportunities*, report of a working party (London: RCP, 2001), available at http://213.146.153.131/pubs/books/womenmed/ (accessed 2 June 2006).

26 Association of Women Solicitors.

27 H Thorne, *Journey to Priesthood: An in-depth study of the first women priests in the Church of England*, Centre for Comparative Studies in Religion and Gender Research Monograph 5 (Bristol: University of Bristol, CCSRG, 2000).

28 S Childs, *New Labour's Women MPs: Women representing women* (Oxford: Routledge, 2004).

29 Ibid.

30 Greed, 'Women in the construction professions'.

31 J Laurance, 'The medical timebomb: "too many women doctors"', *Independent*,

2 Aug 2004.

32 'New women priests to outnumber men for the first time', *Daily Telegraph*, 27 Sept 2004.

33 Royal Institute of British Architects, 'Why do women leave architecture?', RIBA, July 2003.

34 Association of Women Solicitors.

35 She finally gained a medical degree from the University of Paris in 1870, see http://en.wikipedia.org/wiki/Elizabeth_Garrett_Anderson (accessed 2 June 2006).

36 E Cruickshank (ed), *Women and the Law: Strategic career management* (London: Law Society, 2003).

17. Strengthening professionalism

Ethical competence as a path towards the public good

Andy Friedman

Introduction

The supply of professional services is viewed as a problem by the UK government. 'I don't see why consumers should not be able to get legal services as easily as they can buy a tin of beans,' said Department of Constitutional Affairs Minister, Bridget Prentice in October 2005.[1]

One 'solution path' is to try to make the market for professional services like that of other goods, primarily by removing what are regarded as monopolistic barriers to competition. A different path is for the professions themselves to improve their own practice, their own professionalism, based on the development of knowledge, competence and ethical standards and the regulation of these standards through professional bodies – the path of ethical competence.

The market path is being pursued vigorously through the Office of Fair Trading (OFT) and seems to be the dominant path for the current government.[2] In contrast, the ethical competence path relies on education and training providers, professional associations and professionals themselves, demanding a certain kind of support from government:

O   light-touch regulatory institutions or advice to support self-regulation by the professions

○ encouraging professional associations to improve their practice by supporting efforts to learn from each other and to support good practice when it emerges.

The former policy is being pursued patchily through the Better Regulation Commission and the Privy Council, but the latter, of encouraging professional associations to move themselves further along the ethical competence path, seems hardly to have been perceived as a possibility by the current government.

Crucially, governments can pursue both market and ethical competence paths together. In doing so, their task is to strike a balance between the two – unchecked, each can undermine the other. Ethical competence is not a solution of last resort; it protects clients and improves services. To exploit its full potential, professional associations and government must do more.

Rationale for market and ethical competence paths

The idea that professional services should resemble tins of beans reflects the current government's 'choice agenda'. Choice of providers in relation to public services is expected to improve consumer welfare on two grounds. First, it will allow people to take control over their lives and, second, subsequent competition among service providers will lead to reduced costs and innovation. The same argument was applied to professional services by the OFT.[3]

The ethical competence path is a different way to achieve consumer benefit, particularly consumer protection. Ethical competence is based on the idea that professionalism is different from expertise or 'simple competence'. Four elements are instilled as part of professional training and membership of a professional community of practice:

○ knowledge
○ capacity to apply specific knowledge elements in practice circumstances
○ competence: the ability to know when and how to draw

on parts of one's knowledge repertoire and when to forbear from application technically (what will 'work' and what will 'not work')

○ ethical competence: the ability to apply knowledge in an ethical manner as defined by codes of conduct promulgated through professional associations.

This path requires sufficient institutions for training and retraining potential and existing professionals. Policies and programmes for initial qualifications, and recently also for continuing professional development or CPD,[4] need to be put in place and monitored, usually by the professional association (though for initial qualifications this is usually in partnership with universities and colleges). Sometimes this involves on-the-job training leading to exams such as articling in law, residency in medicine and placements in accounting. At this point, the ethics of professional practice are instilled. This is done by promulgating ethical codes and formal training in ethics of professional practice, usually through the use of case studies of dilemmas experienced by practitioners. Members of the profession are also made aware of complaints and disciplinary procedures administered by their professional association or other regulatory body.

The special nature of professional services

In truth, professional services cannot be provided like a tin of beans. There will always be 'information asymmetries' between professionals and consumers. Clients are vulnerable because they do not know which professionals available for hire are competent and ethical (what economists call the problem of 'adverse selection') and they lack the information to judge whether the professional they have hired is doing a good job ('moral hazard' for economists).[5] The severity of these problems varies considerably among professions, but their existence underpins the professional status of any occupational group.

In part these problems occur because, unlike many retail services that involve the frequent provision of products, professional services are provided over a period of time. What occurs during that time can rarely be predicted in detail because it involves human interaction. As a result, there will always be an element of discretion in how the interaction proceeds on the part of the professional (and to a much lesser extent by the client). It is this which demands a form of regulation that is more intimate and more reliant on ethical competence.

Ultimately the quality and value of the service cannot be ensured by alternative sources of supply. Tins of beans are inexpensive, purchased repeatedly and consumers are well able to choose which of the many available brands are best for them. In contrast, professional services have none of these characteristics.

Choosing a 'good' lawyer (or doctor or engineering consultant or auditor) is not made much easier by there being many available in the phone book. By and large most people use particular professional services rarely and struggle to evaluate the quality of the services they receive. Assurances concerning these factors must, in the end, rely on the ethical behaviour of professionals.

Limitations of the ethical competence path

The dangers of going too far down the ethical competence path are well known. The most significant is that it relies on the trustworthiness of professionals. Most sociologists of the professions see professionalism as being 'deployed' to professionals' own benefit. Occupational groups are seen as pursuing 'the professional project'[6] to control markets and achieve material and status benefits and competing among themselves about jurisdictions over particular sectors.[7]

While there is an element of truth in this critique, it neglects the real constraints and characteristics of certain services. Information problems associated with professional services are real and they affect power relations between professionals and clients. Client vulnerability will change over time and between different types of clients. The knowledge base will change, as will the accessibility of information both to professionals and to clients. Nevertheless there will always be areas of modern life that are complex and uncertain in which clients need the protection afforded them by professional ethics. Indeed, these are likely to grow with globalisation and social interconnectedness.

However, the effectiveness of the ethical competence path is limited by problems of professional culture and regulation. Many cases have been highlighted in the media where commitment to ethical competence has taken second place to personal gratification, protection of colleagues or fear of organisational reprisals. Ethical competence does not come automatically with the achievement of credentials. It must be continually reinforced by individual professionals submitting themselves to continuing professional development and self-reflection on ethics and competence. This path also requires vigilance, resources and institutional support, particularly from professional associations.

Limitations of the market path

Milton Friedman argued that anybody claiming to be able to provide a service should be allowed to do so, on the presumption that when they fail, they will lose their reputation, so that only good practitioners will remain in the market.[8] The flaw in this argument is the damage that is done by these failures. What potential customers may well prefer instead is to know that whoever they actually choose will provide a service that will not fall below a certain standard: that they will receive ethical competence; that they will receive a service they can trust and rely on. The more dependent customers are on the service – the more fundamental the service is to their wellbeing, the more dire the consequences of receiving an inadequate service, and the more urgently they believe they need that service – the more they will want whatever service they first encounter to be reliable and trustworthy.

For complex services of this kind, the market path may involve attempts to commoditise a service or to break professional monopolies over its delivery. However, for the services for which clients are most dependent on professionals, both of these strategies are of limited effectiveness. Professional services can be commoditised so that they are more like tins of beans. For example, it is possible to package aspects of these services into 'products' and 'sell' them separately, but many will not be satisfied with an off-the-shelf product because they are more difficult to tailor to their needs. Equally, this inflexibility across whole sectors can hamstring services in adapting to changing circumstances. What is more, the illusion that a professional service is simply a commodity can actually enhance the freedom of professional interpretation.

Seeking to break professional monopolies can also often be self-defeating. At the margins, certain training requirements may be curtailed without damaging service quality. However, as training diminishes, greater and greater supervision is needed and frontline staff become less able to exercise high-quality professional judgement. As a result, breaking monopolies in this way risks damage to flexibility, service quality or efficiency.

More generally, it is increasingly argued that the kinds of market failure in complex professional services, to which the ethical path offers solutions, are a thing of the past. Clearly people can make efforts to become more informed. Use of services leads to improved knowledge of what is available and what are the implications of using the service in terms of side effects and links to deep-seated needs. The internet has added tremendously to the information available on services and the effects of various options people can choose. However, there is still the problem that past experience is of limited use when services needed are specialised and infrequently required. The internet has a great deal of information, but the more information that is available, the greater is the problem of sorting accurate and useful information from spam.

Conclusion

The professions appear to have become complacent in following the ethical competence path. Continuing professional development has come to be taken seriously by professional bodies only since the 1980s and it is still relatively new to many. Ethical codes had been written in outdated language and were inaccessible to the general public. However, there are signs that professional associations are becoming aware of past shortcomings and are responding to pressures from clients, government and the media. Most of the 129 UK professional bodies surveyed by the Professional Associations Research Network (PARN) have been reviewing their ethical codes, their CPD policies and their governance procedures in the past few years.[9] The professions need to pursue the path of ethical competence more vigorously and to campaign collectively to educate the public of the value of professionalism in general.

Government too needs to recognise the full potential of the ethical path. It should employ greater ethics-based regulation to ensure that all professional services are good services and it should support and encourage professional associations to help to make this possible.

Andy Friedman is Director of PARN and Professor of Management and Economics at the University of Bristol.

Notes

1   'Legal advice will be just like buying a tin of beans', *Daily Telegraph*, 18 Oct 2005.
2   Office of Fair Trading, *Competition in Professions* (London: OFT, 2001).
3   Ibid.
4   AL Friedman et al, *Continuing Professional Development in the UK: Policies and programmes* (Bristol: PARN, 2000).
5   E Fama and M Jensen, 'Separation of ownership and control', *Journal of Law and Economics* 26 (1983).
6   MS Larson, *The Rise of Professionalism: A sociological analysis* (Berkeley, CA: University of California, 1977).
7   A Abbott, *The System of the Professions* (Chicago: University of Chicago, 1988).
8   M Friedman, *Capitalism and Freedom* (Chicago: University of Chicago, 1962).
9   A Friedman and J Mason, *The Professionalisation of UK Professional Associations: Governance, management and member relations* (Bristol: PARN, 2004).

18. Good work and professional work

Richard Reeves and John Knell

Britain entered the twentieth century as an industrial society; it began the twenty-first as a professional one. The power and status of professional groups – in the private and then public sectors – have increased dramatically over the last hundred years. Some professions, largely those in the state sector, are now seen to be threatened by a combination of central government regulations and consumer expectations. But professional strength is still one of the dominant facts of our culture today, and any analysis of the future of professionalism must grapple with its history. Professional power is not waning, at least not yet. But the basis of that power is shifting; the balance between the defining characteristics of professional is altering, and must alter. Professionals are being led back to an older, richer definition of what it is that they 'profess' to offer the rest of us in exchange for their status. Ethics and impact will come to predominate over expertise and market capture in the definition of professional labour. Good work is what defines professionalism.

Professional life is intimately entwined with economic, social and political power. Professions form many of the main battalions in societal conflict: the protagonists in twenty-first-century power struggles are very much more likely to be competing professional groups (managers versus doctors, accountants versus regulators, civil servants versus journalists) than economically defined social classes. The (recent) history of society is the history of professional struggle.

As the social historian Harold Perkin points out, ecologies of power shaped by professions are more complex, and more attractive, than 'a class society in the traditional sense of a binary model with a small ruling class exploiting a large underclass, but a collection of parallel hierarchies of unequal height, each with its own ladder of many rungs'.[1]

In a professional society, status, power and income flow from demonstrable possession of human capital. As such, it is more meritocratic than one in which inherited wealth in the form of land or accumulated financial capital is the primary source of power – although, as Perkin points out, 'merit' is more easily acquired by some.

The 'free' market is of course highly professionalised. The rules and regulations necessary for capitalism have reinforced the power bases of accountants, bankers and lawyers, as well as spawning a whole range of new professions: human resources, risk management and training. Management itself has been steadily professionalised, with MBAs or other qualifications increasingly required for upward mobility.

Postwar social democracy created the conditions for a new burst of profession-building. Some professions, such as social work, were brought into existence by the welfare state. Many more saw a significant numerical expansion and increased power: civil servants, doctors, nurses, police officers and teachers. Increasingly, professionals were divided by their position in relation to the market and the state and also by their attitude to the role and scope of government. 'The bifurcation of the professional ideal', writes Perkin, 'reflected the splitting of the professional class into two warring factions.'[2] Of course many professions crossed the public–private divide (everyone needs lawyers). But the two branches of the professional class have generally been at loggerheads, especially since 1979. Money is a good part of the struggle. Private sector professionals create wealth; public sector professionals spend it. Where then should resources be focused?

But this war, which has survived the Thatcherite period, has obscured the features shared by professions in both spheres: an increasing emphasis on qualifications, tightening regulation and regimes of inspection and a high degree of control over the supply of services. Professions can define themselves, and the source of their power, in four principal ways.

First, by the erection of narrow gates of entry into the labour market for the provision of services. Formal qualifications are the principal mechanism by which the professions are able to control the supply of labour into their area of activity: PGCE, MD, LLB, ACCA ONE or Dip. Soc. Work. At the same time, of course, these qualifications provide assurance to the consumer that the professional has an idea of what they are doing. The basis of professional power here is an asymmetry in knowledge, skills and expertise between them and the user of their services. Much of this human capital is out of sight of the user – it is often unnecessary to know how the accountant tallied the books, or what the detail of company law is or the precise biochemical pathology of a disease. In this sense, professionalisation is simply a formalised version of the division of labour. The fact that their expertise lies in a 'black box', invisible to laypeople (and we are all laypeople now), becomes an issue when the application of expertise has a profound impact on individuals themselves. Health and education are obvious examples: Why do I need that test? Why are you teaching my child to read in that weird 'phonic' way?

On top of the formal entry gates, professions often erect informal defences at their occupational boundaries: lawyers and doctors love to use Latin, academics are partial to often unnecessary jargon, the Foreign and Commonwealth Office has had a long history of requiring the right sort of accent for embassy cocktail parties. This second line of defence, resting on mystification, is declining in the light of greater public knowledge and a renewed push towards meritocracy. But the qualification gates are narrowing, and becoming more widespread. In a number of occupations, postgraduate qualifications or diplomas are becoming necessary, often as a result of tougher state regulation: childcare is a good example of an area of work that is being professionalised in this way (notwithstanding the still sizeable gap between the UK and our European neighbours in this specific regard).

The second potential defining characteristic of a profession is the collective organisation of labour. Having established the qualifications required to trade, the next step is to act together to maximise the profession's political and economic leverage. Trade bodies act as often powerful voices for the interests of a profession. Some professions, such as teachers and hospital workers, act through trade unions – although these act as quasi-professional associations. But the greatest power is wielded not by unions but by associations, colleges and societies: the Law Society, Royal College of Nursing, Bar Association and British Medical Association. These bodies act not only for the economic and occupational interests of their members, but ostensibly also for the users of their services. (Inevitably the line is blurred.) As Perkin points out: 'Profession came to mean an occupation which so effectively controlled its labour market that it never had to behave like a trade union.'[3] Because any individual who wishes to practise in these professions is usually obliged to join the relevant association, the professions have managed to operate something very close to a 'closed shop', long since abolished for everyone else. The power of professional associations is further enhanced when there is effectively a single employer to negotiate with, such as the NHS: monopoly meets monopsony.

The third defining characteristic of a profession is a set of shared values by which their work is conducted: a professional ethos. The distinguishing characteristic of the professional here is not their formal expertise, but their motivation. Here what makes the professional is not what they know, but *how* they work. In some occupations the professional ethic is explicit: the Hippocratic oath is the exemplar. But in most professions the ethic is informally accumulated over a long period of time, often based on unspoken assumptions on the part of both users and providers of services. Lawyers don't lie, nurses 'care' not just for the body but for the person, civil servants remain politically neutral. Needless to say there is an abundance of exceptions to these ethical imperatives, but they cut against the grain. The attachment of ethical standards to certain positions is not restricted to paid work, or professions of course: when a woman lied about a car accident, and got some children in her care to lie on her behalf, it was a national story only because she was a scout leader.[4] Who would be shocked if a politician, management consultant or advertising executive were found to have uttered an untruth?

The professional identifier of a shared ethic is older than the identifiers of qualification screening and occupational capture. The very term 'professional', in its original sense, carries a vocational, motivational import. Individuals entering religious orders were required to take an oath, to 'profess' their faith and commitment to their vocation and those entering other occupations were expected to 'declare publicly' (*profitieri*) both their skills and their character for the job. Professional ethics can conflict with self-interest, especially in a market economy. It may be better for the individual professional to undertake more work than necessary, prescribe a different drug, be economical with the truth. These are the moments when professional integrity is tested. But a general sense of trust that the members of a profession will act in accordance with its ethos is a vital component in its maintenance of social and economic status.

The final identifier of a professional is the impact of their work. This is most clearly the case with the provision of services, largely in the state sector. A teacher may have a PGCE, the National Union of Teachers may act effectively to secure her monopsonistic advantage, and she may have a strong motivation to equip the next generation for a fulfilling life. But she also has to succeed: the children in the classroom have to be educated. And in other professions, the same need for impact is clear: the patient is healed; the vulnerable family is supported. There is a transformative element to professional work. If the third characteristic is the 'how', this last defining feature is the 'what'. In the Nick Hornby novel, *How to be Good*, a GP is threatened by the apparent success of an untrained, hippy healer. She is struggling to see how she could define what he actually does. But she realises that if she restricts herself to a simple description of impact, the problem disappears: he makes sick people better. In the old days, that is how people saw doctors. Now they are highly qualified, highly regulated experts operating in a specific, clearly demarcated occupational and institutional space. And health care is much the better for all this. But the final impact of their work is what matters most.

For most of the second half of the twentieth century professional status and authority was built on the first two identifiers – assessed expertise and occupational capture. Both of these are being eroded. The informational asymmetry between professional and citizen is being reduced by rising educational standards and the greater accessibility of information, especially on the internet. A patient can become more expert than most GPs on a specific condition after half an hour in front of their computer. Although the reduction of the informational advantage is greatest in taxpayer-funded services, it is occurring elsewhere too. I can download my own will and testament, or tenancy agreement. Spreadsheets, once the preserve of finance professionals, can be used with ease by every decently educated 15-year-old.

The growing knowledge and confidence of the users of professional services requires a profound shift in the nature of professional labour. Increasingly professionals will be expected not merely to provide a service, but to act in partnership with the user in the construction of a service: they will, in the new jargon, have to become 'co-producers'. In some cases, such as the generalist GP, their specific knowledge may be limited, and even less than that of the user. But they are able to offer advice based on their wisdom, judgement and knowledge of the health care system. This makes them no less valuable to the patient, but it does shift the basis of valuation away from pure expertise.

At the same time, the carefully defended borders of occupational privilege are under steady assault. Barristers were unable to stop moves to allow solicitors to speak in court. Paralegals can undertake much of the work once done by lawyers. The medical profession has run a better defence, but nurse practitioners are now on the loose, and once their blindingly obvious value and cost-effectiveness can no longer be shrouded, further gains into traditional doctor territory are sure to be made. Teaching assistants are able to do what only teachers could once do. Restrictions on necessary qualifications for stockbroking have been loosened.

To secure their position, the professions should not engage in futile attempts to prevent these dynamic processes. They should instead strengthen the other sources of professional status and authority – the ethos guiding their work, and its transforming impact on the world around them. As Tom Brown's schoolmaster insisted:

> You talk of 'working to get your living' and 'doing some real good in the world' in the same breath. Now you may be getting a good living in a profession, and yet not doing any good at all in the world . . . keep the latter before you as a holy object, and you will be right, whether you make a living or not; but if you dwell on the other, you'll very likely drop into mere money-making.[5]

Professional identity has been based on good qualifications and good collective organisation. In the future it will need to be based more securely on good work. Good work is work undertaken with integrity as well as competence. A professional is someone who is demonstrably good at what they do, but also doing it against a set of fixed ethical benchmarks that the user can trust. Work, whether paid or unpaid, is the principal means by which we impact on the world. It is a transforming process. Good work consists of efforts to transform the world or the people around us in a positive direction. Good professional work additionally involves the exercise of a set of specific skills. This is where trends in professional identification coincide with a growing demand among individuals for work that is 'meaningful'.[6]

In their book, *Good Work: When excellence and ethics meet*, Howard Gardner, Mihaly Csikszentmihalyi and William Damon write that people who are doing good work – according to their definition, where 'excellence and ethics meet' – are those who are 'thoughtful about their responsibilities and the *implications* of their work' (our emphasis).[7]

The necessary and positive processes of meritocracy and information-sharing are chipping away at the Mount Olympus model of professionalism. The professions need to re-connect with the deeper roots of their authority: why, how and to what end they do their work. Good work begets professionalism, and the future of the professions is dependent on their ability to remake and refashion good work.

Richard Reeves and John Knell are co-directors of Intelligence Agency, an ideas consultancy.

Notes

1   H Perkin, *The Rise of Professional Society* (London: Routledge, 2002).
2   Ibid.
3   Ibid.
4   See www.guardian.co.uk/crime/article/0,,1749623,00.html (accessed 26 May 2006).
5   Quoted in M Wiener, *English Culture and the Decline of the Industrial Spirit, 1850–1980* (Cambridge: Cambridge University Press, 1981).
6   See J Knell and R Reeves, *Transforming Work* (forthcoming).
7   H Gardner, M Csikszentmihalyi and W Damon, *Good Work: When excellence and ethics meet* (New York: Basic Books, 2001).

DEMOS – Licence to Publish

THE WORK (AS DEFINED BELOW) IS PROVIDED UNDER THE TERMS OF THIS LICENCE ("LICENCE"). THE WORK IS PROTECTED BY COPYRIGHT AND/OR OTHER APPLICABLE LAW. ANY USE OF THE WORK OTHER THAN AS AUTHORIZED UNDER THIS LICENCE IS PROHIBITED. BY EXERCISING ANY RIGHTS TO THE WORK PROVIDED HERE, YOU ACCEPT AND AGREE TO BE BOUND BY THE TERMS OF THIS LICENCE. DEMOS GRANTS YOU THE RIGHTS CONTAINED HERE IN CONSIDERATION OF YOUR ACCEPTANCE OF SUCH TERMS AND CONDITIONS.

1. **Definitions**
   a **"Collective Work"** means a work, such as a periodical issue, anthology or encyclopedia, in which the Work in its entirety in unmodified form, along with a number of other contributions, constituting separate and independent works in themselves, are assembled into a collective whole. A work that constitutes a Collective Work will not be considered a Derivative Work (as defined below) for the purposes of this Licence.
   b **"Derivative Work"** means a work based upon the Work or upon the Work and other pre-existing works, such as a musical arrangement, dramatization, fictionalization, motion picture version, sound recording, art reproduction, abridgment, condensation, or any other form in which the Work may be recast, transformed, or adapted, except that a work that constitutes a Collective Work or a translation from English into another language will not be considered a Derivative Work for the purpose of this Licence.
   c **"Licensor"** means the individual or entity that offers the Work under the terms of this Licence.
   d **"Original Author"** means the individual or entity who created the Work.
   e **"Work"** means the copyrightable work of authorship offered under the terms of this Licence.
   f **"You"** means an individual or entity exercising rights under this Licence who has not previously violated the terms of this Licence with respect to the Work, or who has received express permission from DEMOS to exercise rights under this Licence despite a previous violation.
2. **Fair Use Rights.** Nothing in this licence is intended to reduce, limit, or restrict any rights arising from fair use, first sale or other limitations on the exclusive rights of the copyright owner under copyright law or other applicable laws.
3. **Licence Grant.** Subject to the terms and conditions of this Licence, Licensor hereby grants You a worldwide, royalty-free, non-exclusive, perpetual (for the duration of the applicable copyright) licence to exercise the rights in the Work as stated below:
   a to reproduce the Work, to incorporate the Work into one or more Collective Works, and to reproduce the Work as incorporated in the Collective Works;
   b to distribute copies or phonorecords of, display publicly, perform publicly, and perform publicly by means of a digital audio transmission the Work including as incorporated in Collective Works;
   The above rights may be exercised in all media and formats whether now known or hereafter devised. The above rights include the right to make such modifications as are technically necessary to exercise the rights in other media and formats. All rights not expressly granted by Licensor are hereby reserved.
4. **Restrictions.** The licence granted in Section 3 above is expressly made subject to and limited by the following restrictions:
   a You may distribute, publicly display, publicly perform, or publicly digitally perform the Work only under the terms of this Licence, and You must include a copy of, or the Uniform Resource Identifier for, this Licence with every copy or phonorecord of the Work You distribute, publicly display, publicly perform, or publicly digitally perform. You may not offer or impose any terms on the Work that alter or restrict the terms of this Licence or the recipients' exercise of the rights granted hereunder. You may not sublicence the Work. You must keep intact all notices that refer to this Licence and to the disclaimer of warranties. You may not distribute, publicly display, publicly perform, or publicly digitally perform the Work with any technological measures that control access or use of the Work in a manner inconsistent with the terms of this Licence Agreement. The above applies to the Work as incorporated in a Collective Work, but this does not require the Collective Work apart from the Work itself to be made subject to the terms of this Licence. If You create a Collective Work, upon notice from any Licencor You must, to the extent practicable, remove from the Collective Work any reference to such Licensor or the Original Author, as requested.
   b You may not exercise any of the rights granted to You in Section 3 above in any manner that is primarily intended for or directed toward commercial advantage or private monetary

compensation. The exchange of the Work for other copyrighted works by means of digital file-sharing or otherwise shall not be considered to be intended for or directed toward commercial advantage or private monetary compensation, provided there is no payment of any monetary compensation in connection with the exchange of copyrighted works.

c   If you distribute, publicly display, publicly perform, or publicly digitally perform the Work or any Collective Works, You must keep intact all copyright notices for the Work and give the Original Author credit reasonable to the medium or means You are utilizing by conveying the name (or pseudonym if applicable) of the Original Author if supplied; the title of the Work if supplied. Such credit may be implemented in any reasonable manner; provided, however, that in the case of a Collective Work, at a minimum such credit will appear where any other comparable authorship credit appears and in a manner at least as prominent as such other comparable authorship credit.

5. Representations, Warranties and Disclaimer

a   By offering the Work for public release under this Licence, Licensor represents and warrants that, to the best of Licensor's knowledge after reasonable inquiry:

  i   Licensor has secured all rights in the Work necessary to grant the licence rights hereunder and to permit the lawful exercise of the rights granted hereunder without You having any obligation to pay any royalties, compulsory licence fees, residuals or any other payments;

  ii The Work does not infringe the copyright, trademark, publicity rights, common law rights or any other right of any third party or constitute defamation, invasion of privacy or other tortious injury to any third party.

b   EXCEPT AS EXPRESSLY STATED IN THIS LICENCE OR OTHERWISE AGREED IN WRITING OR REQUIRED BY APPLICABLE LAW, THE WORK IS LICENCED ON AN "AS IS" BASIS, WITHOUT WARRANTIES OF ANY KIND, EITHER EXPRESS OR IMPLIED INCLUDING, WITHOUT LIMITATION, ANY WARRANTIES REGARDING THE CONTENTS OR ACCURACY OF THE WORK.

6. Limitation on Liability. EXCEPT TO THE EXTENT REQUIRED BY APPLICABLE LAW, AND EXCEPT FOR DAMAGES ARISING FROM LIABILITY TO A THIRD PARTY RESULTING FROM BREACH OF THE WARRANTIES IN SECTION 5, IN NO EVENT WILL LICENSOR BE LIABLE TO YOU ON ANY LEGAL THEORY FOR ANY SPECIAL, INCIDENTAL, CONSEQUENTIAL, PUNITIVE OR EXEMPLARY DAMAGES ARISING OUT OF THIS LICENCE OR THE USE OF THE WORK, EVEN IF LICENSOR HAS BEEN ADVISED OF THE POSSIBILITY OF SUCH DAMAGES.

7. Termination

a   This Licence and the rights granted hereunder will terminate automatically upon any breach by You of the terms of this Licence. Individuals or entities who have received Collective Works from You under this Licence, however, will not have their licences terminated provided such individuals or entities remain in full compliance with those licences. Sections 1, 2, 5, 6, 7, and 8 will survive any termination of this Licence.

b   Subject to the above terms and conditions, the licence granted here is perpetual (for the duration of the applicable copyright in the Work). Notwithstanding the above, Licensor reserves the right to release the Work under different licence terms or to stop distributing the Work at any time; provided, however that any such election will not serve to withdraw this Licence (or any other licence that has been, or is required to be, granted under the terms of this Licence), and this Licence will continue in full force and effect unless terminated as stated above.

8. Miscellaneous

a   Each time You distribute or publicly digitally perform the Work or a Collective Work, DEMOS offers to the recipient a licence to the Work on the same terms and conditions as the licence granted to You under this Licence.

b   If any provision of this Licence is invalid or unenforceable under applicable law, it shall not affect the validity or enforceability of the remainder of the terms of this Licence, and without further action by the parties to this agreement, such provision shall be reformed to the minimum extent necessary to make such provision valid and enforceable.

c   No term or provision of this Licence shall be deemed waived and no breach consented to unless such waiver or consent shall be in writing and signed by the party to be charged with such waiver or consent.

d   This Licence constitutes the entire agreement between the parties with respect to the Work licensed here. There are no understandings, agreements or representations with respect to the Work not specified here. Licensor shall not be bound by any additional provisions that may appear in any communication from You. This Licence may not be modified without the mutual written agreement of DEMOS and You.